William S. Ferguson

Junior Songs

a collection of sacred hymns and songs

William S. Ferguson

Junior Songs
a collection of sacred hymns and songs

ISBN/EAN: 9783337089795

Printed in Europe, USA, Canada, Australia, Japan

Cover: Foto ©Lupo / pixelio.de

More available books at **www.hansebooks.com**

JUNIOR SONGS:

A COLLECTION OF

SACRED HYMNS AND SONGS,

FOR USE IN

Meetings of Junior Societies, Sunday Schools, etc.

COMMITTEE ON SELECTIONS:

WM. S. FERGUSON, ISRAEL P. BLACK.

MUSICAL EDITORS:

JOHN R. SWENEY, WM. J. KIRKPATRICK

PHILADELPHIA:

Published by JOHN J. HOOD, 1024 Arch St.

PREFACE.

Realizing the need of a suitable collection of Hymns and Sacred Songs for the use of the Boys and Girls of the Junior Department of the Christian Endeavor Societies, and the Epworth Leagues; the Philadelphia Union of Junior Christian Endeavor Societies selected a committee to compile this volume under the title of JUNIOR SONGS. The committee has been actuated by a strong desire to present the very best collection of hymns that it was possible to obtain.

A large proportion of the Hymns and Tunes have been expressly written for JUNIOR SONGS, to which has been added many of the most popular and useful hymns of the day.

Much attention has been bestowed upon selecting such tunes as were attractive and within the compass of youthful voices; at the same time great care has been exercised in selecting such hymns as teach spiritual and evangelical truths. Believing in the early conversion of the young to Christ, we have endeavored to place such songs in their mouths as, becoming fastened upon their hearts, may lead them to early seek and find the blessed Saviour. At the request of many a few selections for Responsive Readings for use at the Junior Meetings have been selected and can be used in such a manner as may be deemed advisable.

We believe that this unsurpassed collection of Hymns will meet a want in the Junior Work which is so rapidly developing in every part of the world; and it is the earnest prayer of the committee that JUNIOR SONGS may be the means of awakening a greater interest in the work among the Boys and Girls, and implanting in their hearts a strong desire to do something for "Christ and his church."

On behalf of the committee,

WILLIAM S. FERGUSON.
ISRAEL P. BLACK.

JUNIOR SONGS.

Let Us Stand for Christ.

A. W. S. — Rev. A. W. Spooner.

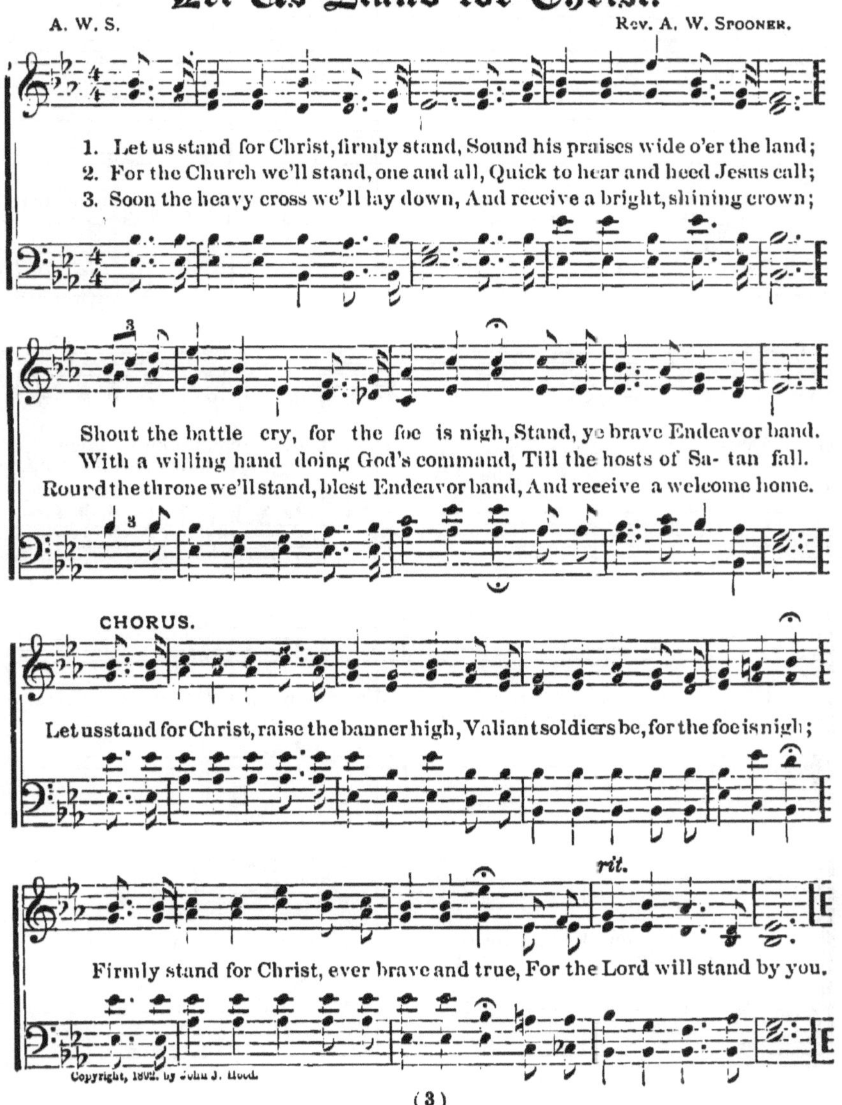

1. Let us stand for Christ, firmly stand, Sound his praises wide o'er the land;
2. For the Church we'll stand, one and all, Quick to hear and heed Jesus call;
3. Soon the heavy cross we'll lay down, And receive a bright, shining crown;
Shout the battle cry, for the foe is nigh, Stand, ye brave Endeavor band.
With a willing hand doing God's command, Till the hosts of Sa- tan fall.
Round the throne we'll stand, blest Endeavor band, And receive a welcome home.
CHORUS.
Let us stand for Christ, raise the banner high, Valiant soldiers be, for the foe is nigh;
rit.
Firmly stand for Christ, ever brave and true, For the Lord will stand by you.

The Apostles' Creed.

Wm. J Kirkpatrick.

I believe in God the Father Almighty,
Maker of heaven and earth:
And in Jesus Christ his only Son our Lord;
Who was conceived by the Holy Ghost,
Born of the Virgin Mary;
Suffered under Pontius Pilate,
Was crucified, dead, and buried;
The third day he rose from the dead;
He ascended into heaven,
And sitteth on the right hand of God the Father Almighty;
From thence he shall come to judge
The quick and the dead.
I believe in the Holy Ghost;
The holy catholic Church;
The communion of saints;
The forgiveness of sins;
The resurrection of the body,
And the life everlasting.
rit.
A - men, a - - men.

Welcome to Our Number.

E. E. Hewitt. Jno. R. Sweney.

1. Welcome to our number, Happy welcome, friends! True and kindly greeting
2. Welcome, for we need you, Need your words to cheer; Jesus needs your service,
3. In the strength of Je- sus You our pledge will take, Making each endeavor
Ev - 'ry heart extends. Come, our hands to strengthen, Come, our ranks to swell,
And your love sin- cere. We can help each other, Marching side by side,
For his precious sake; As our Eld- er Brother He will ev - er stand,
Living now for Jesus, Come, his love to tell.
Ever drawing nearer To our blessed Guide.
Crown our humble efforts, Bless his trusting band.
CHORUS.
Welcome, welcome, happy, happy
welcome! True and kindly greeting Ev'ry heart extends; One in Christ our Saviour,
May his tender fa - vor Rest up- on us sweetly While our song ascends.

Hold Up the Bible.

E. E. Hewitt. Wm. J. Kirkpatrick.

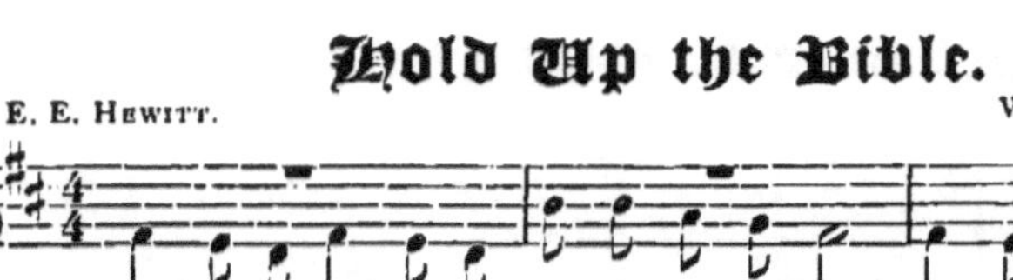

1. Hold up the Bi- ble, for on- ly there we learn, Good news for sinners, the
2. Hold up the Bi- ble, a lamp to guide our way, All thro' the journey, with
3. Hold up the Bi- ble, with brave and loyal hand, Guard well the treasure, the
4. Hold up the Bi- ble, there's gold in every line, Bright gems of promise on

gen- tle word "re- turn;" Book of sal- va- tion, a gift from God a- bove,
pure and heavenly ray; Showing the dangers that lurk on ev- ery side,
hope of this our land; Let not the scof- fer e'er ban- ish from our youth,
all its pag- es shine; "Sweeter than honey" the comfort it bestows,

Let us ev- er prize it—the let-ter of his love. Hold up the Bi- ble!
And a mighty stronghold, wherein the soul may hide.
Wisdom ev- erlast- ing—the holy book of truth.
There, in blessed beauty, blooms Sharon's lovely Rose.

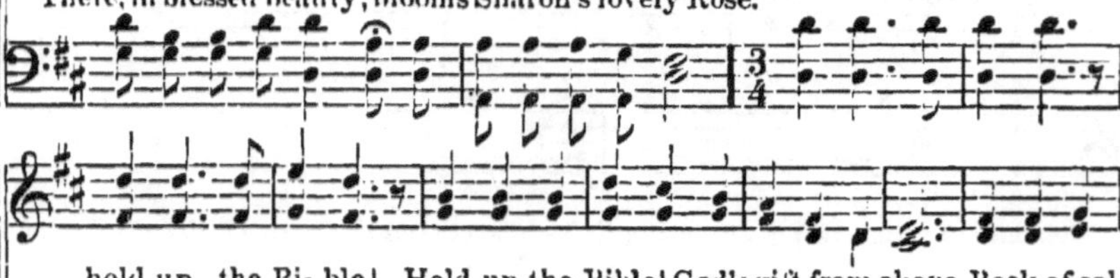

hold up the Bi- ble! Hold up the Bible! God's gift from above, Book of sal-

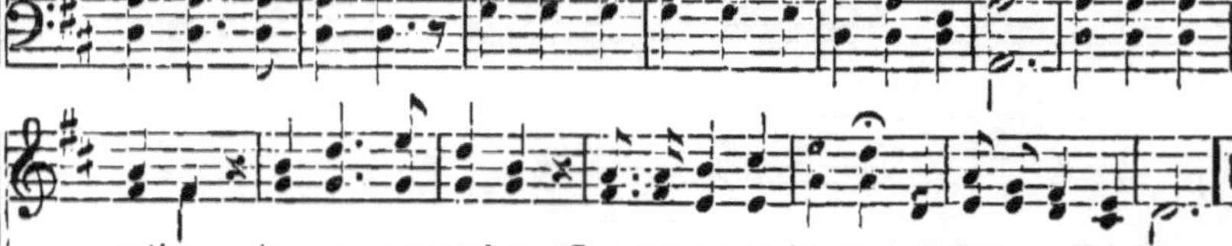

vation to ev- ery nation. Let us ever prize it—the letter of his love.

"This I did for Thee." 7

H. Bonar. W. H. Doane.

Slow.
1. I gave my life for thee, My precious blood I shed, That thou might'st ransom'd be,
2. I spent long years for thee In weariness and woe, That one e- ter- ni - ty
3. My Father's house of light, My rainbow-circled throne, I left for earthly night,
4. I suffered much for thee,—More than my tongue can tell, Of bitterest agony;
And quickened from the dead; I gave my life for thee; What hast thou done for me?
Of joy thou mightest know; I spent long years for thee; Hast thou spent one for me?
For wand'rings sad and lone; I left it all all for thee; Hast thou left aught for me?
To rescue thee from hell; I suffered much for thee; What dost thou bear for me?
CHORUS.
This I did for thee, What hast thou done for me?
This I did for thee, What hast thou done for me? Yes,
This I did for thee, What hast thou done for me?
this I did for thee,

5 And I have brought to thee,
Down from my house above,
Salvation full and free,
My pardon and my love;
Great gifts I brought to thee;
What hast thou brought to me?

6 Oh, let thy life be given,
Thy years for me be spent,
World fetters all be riven,
And joy with suffering blent;
Give thou thyself to me,
And I will welcome thee!

All His Wondrous Works.

E. E. Hewitt.
Jno. R. Sweney.
1. The robin's car - ol, gay and sweet, Rings down the forest aisle, While
2. The waves that break in snowy lace With ev- 'ry ris - ing tide, The
3. But there is mu- sic, sweeter far Than nature's voi- ces make, Nor
ferns and flow'rs look up to greet The sunbeam's golden smile; And bird, and flow'r,
vines that with their beauty grace
[and
The mountain's rugged side; The tender grass-blades
bird, nor wave, nor circling star In this grand song partake; But christian children
balmy breeze Thro' all the verdant wood, And gentle rustling of the leaves Re-
at our feet, The arching sky a - bove, The blessed, happy tale repeat, They
gladly raise Their hearts to him above, In joyful hymns of grateful praise, They
CHORUS.
mind us, God is good.
tell us God is love.
sing redeeming love.
All his wondrous works proclaim, Great and holy
is his name, Earth, and sea, and heaven above, Praise the Lord, the God of love.
Copyright, 1892, by Jno. R. Sweney.

Bear the Cross for Jesus.

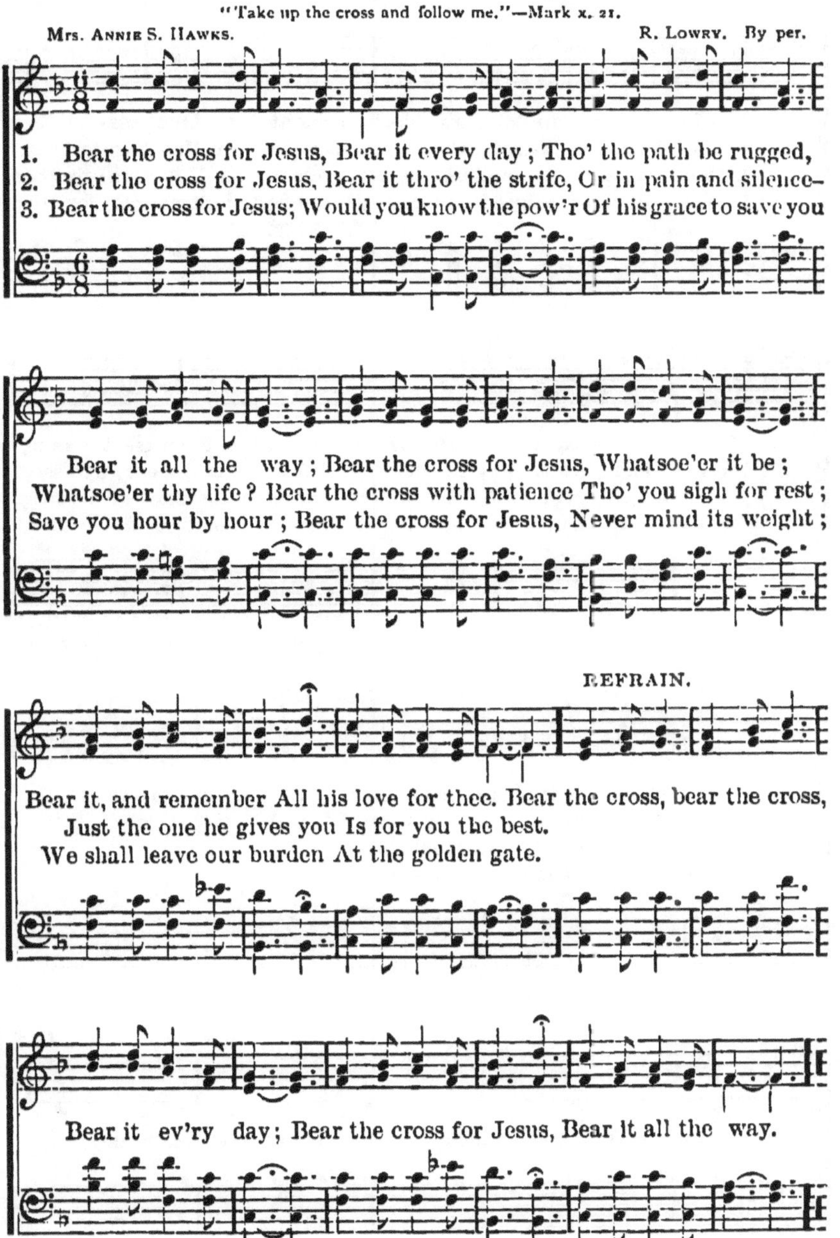
"Take up the cross and follow me."—Mark x. 21.
Mrs. Annie S. Hawks.
R. Lowry. By per.
1. Bear the cross for Jesus, Bear it every day; Tho' the path be rugged,
2. Bear the cross for Jesus, Bear it thro' the strife, Or in pain and silence-
3. Bear the cross for Jesus; Would you know the pow'r Of his grace to save you
Bear it all the way; Bear the cross for Jesus, Whatsoe'er it be;
Whatsoe'er thy life? Bear the cross with patience Tho' you sigh for rest;
Save you hour by hour; Bear the cross for Jesus, Never mind its weight;
REFRAIN.
Bear it, and remember All his love for thee. Bear the cross, bear the cross,
Just the one he gives you Is for you the best.
We shall leave our burden At the golden gate.
Bear it ev'ry day; Bear the cross for Jesus, Bear it all the way.

We All Can Do Good.

Fanny J. Crosby.
Jno. R. Sweney.
1. Our lives, we are told, are but fleet-ing at best, Like ros- es they
2. A look or a smile, that in kindness we give, May com-fort a
3. How ma-ny a-round us are strangers to God, How ma-ny poor
4. We all can do good, and we all can bestow Some gift for the
fade and de - cay; Then let us do good while the present is ours,
des-o-late heart, May sweeten a life that is lone-ly and sad,
children we see; If such we could bring to the foot of the cross,
sake of our Lord; If on-ly a cup of cold wa-ter we give,
D.S.—Re-member the proverb, re-member it now,
Fine.
CHORUS.
Be use-ful as long as we stay. Do good un-to others, do
And hope to the wea-ry im - part.
How grateful and glad we should be.
Our souls will not lose their re - ward.
We all can do good if we try.
they fly;
D.S.
good while we can,—Our moments how quickly [how quick-ly they fly.

From "The Wells of Salvation," by per.

Send out the Sunlight.

Ellen Dare.
Jno. R. Sweney.
1. Send out the sunlight, the sunlight of cheer, Shine on earth's sadness till it disap-
2. Send out the sunlight in letter and word· Speak it and think it till hearts are all
3. Send out the sunlight each hour and day, Crown all the years with its luminous
4. Send out the sunlight that speaks in a smile, Often it shortens the long, weary
pear—Souls are in waiting this message to hear, Send out the sunlight of love.
stirred—Hearts that are hungry for prayers still unheard,
Send out the sunlight of love.
ray, Nourish the seeds that are sown on the way, Send out the sunlight of love.
mile, Often the burdens seem light for awhile, Send out the sunlight of love.
CHORUS.
Send out the sunlight of love, ... Send out the sunlight of love, ...
the sunlight of love,
the sunlight of love,
Send out the sunlight, Send out the sunlight, Send out the sunlight of love.
the sunlight of love.
Copyright, 1892, by Jno. R. Sweney.

5 Send out the sunlight, as free as the air!
Blessings will follow with none to compare, [spair!
Blessings of peace, that will rise from de-
Send out the sunlight of love.

6 Send out the sunlight, you have it in you!
Clouds may obscure it just now from your view; [come true,
Pray for its presence! your prayer will
Send out the sunlight of love.

A Place for Thee.

J. B. Mackay. — Jno. R. Sweney.

Moderato.

1. In realms of bliss, where all is pure, Je- sus has a place for thee;
His blood has made our ti - tle sure, Je- sus has a place for thee.

2. His faithful promise firm- ly stands, Je- sus has a place for thee;
A place prepared by his own hands, Je- sus has a place for thee.

3. Tho' here oppressed with toil and care, Je- sus has a place for thee;
Sweet rest and peace awaits us there, Je- sus has a place for thee.

4. Then praise his great and wond'rous love, Je- sus has a place for thee;
His saints shall reign with him above, Je- sus has a place for thee.

CHORUS.

A place for thee, a place for thee, Je- sus has a place for thee; In his

Father's house where many mansions be, Je- sus has a place for thee.

5 O sinner, come, and seek his face,
Jesus has a place for thee;
His pardon, love, and boundless grace,
Jesus has a place for thee.

6 Whoever seeks a place will find,
Jesus has a place for thee;
There's room enough for all mankind,
Jesus has a place for thee.

Rescue Them.

L. H. Edmunds.
Wm. J. Kirkpatrick.
1. Christian, to the rescue! Hasten souls to save; Lis- ten to the warning,
2. Tar- ry not, nor fal- ter, Souls are in distress; Ea- ger, glad to help them,
3 While the toilers bravely Seek the tempest-tossed, Thro' the dashing breakers,
4. Here's the mighty Captain Standing by our side, Faith, and strength, and courage
Sounding o'er the wave; See the signals fly - ing From the sinking ship;
Who will answer "yes"? Read- y now the life-boat, Be it nobly manned;
Lest a soul be lost,—All who lift pe - ti- tions Shall their labors share,
Free- ly he'll pro- vide; Now a ray of glo - ry Breaks the shadows dim;
Let the cry for helpers Pass from lip to lip.
Earnest, faithful workers, Christ's own loyal band.
hro' the lonely night-watch Prevalent in prayer.
Present, sure salva- tion, Trusting all to him.
CHORUS.
Rescue them, rescue them;
Who will volunteer? In the name of Jesus haste to save and cheer; Rescue them,
rescue them, Christian volunteer,
Strangers, friends, or brothers, Haste to save and cheer.

Sunshine in the Soul.

E. E. Hewitt.
Jno. R. Sweney.
1. There's sunshine in my soul to-day, More glo - ri- ous and bright Than
2. There's mu- sic in my soul to-day, A car - ol to my King, And
3. There's springtime in my soul to-day, For when the Lord is near The
4. There's gladness in my soul to-day, And hope, and praise, and love, For
glows in an - y earthly sky, For Je - sus is my light.
Je - sus, list - ening, can hear The songs I can - not sing.
dove of peace sings in my heart, The flowers of grace ap - pear.
blessings which he gives me now, For joys "laid up" a - bove.
REFRAIN.
Oh, there's sun - - shine, blessed sun - shine, When the peaceful, happy moments
sunshine in the soul, bless - ed sunshine in the soul,
roll; When Jesus shows his smiling face There is sunshine in the soul.
happy moments roll;
Copyright, 1887, by Jno. R. Sweney.

Save One.

E. E Hewitt. — Wm. J. Kirkpatrick.

1. Out in the breakers are per- ish- ing souls, Save one, save one;
2. Out in the darkness of sin's aw- ful night, Save one, save one;
3. Out on the mountain so sad - ly a - stray, Save one, save one;
4. Loved ones or strangers, whoe'er they may be, Save one, save one;
Out where the current of sin mad- ly rolls, Save one, save one.
Tell them of Je - sus, and lead to the light, Save one, save one.
From the sweet home land so far, far a - way, Save one, save one.
Go in his Spir - it who saves you and me, Save one, save one.
CHORUS.
Pit - y the per- ish- ing, La- bor and pray; Hasten to res- cue them,
Save one to-day, Then in your heart will be heaven begun, Save one, save one.

Young Soldiers for Jesus.

JENNIE E. JOHNSON.
JNO. R. SWENEY.
1. Oh, we are young soldiers for Je- sus, And he, our Commander and Friend,
2. Oh, we are young soldiers for Je - sus, And promise to follow him still;
3. Our pathway may sometimes be rugged, Our marching may sometimes be long,
D. S.—we are young soldiers for Je- sus, And he, our Commander and Friend,
Fine.
Will help us each one to be faith-ful, And lead us safe on to the end;
A place in the Sunday-school army To-day we are hap- py to fill;
But glad - ly our footsteps shall ev- er Keep time to the voice of our song;
Will help us each one to be faith-ful, And lead us safe on to the end;
Wherev - er the post of our du - ty Let none of us fal- ter nor fear;
Yes, we are young soldiers for Je - sus, And proudly our colors we show;
And oh, when the warfare is o - ver, And Jesus our Saviour shall come,
Chorus D.S.
Remember no danger can harm us When Jesus our Saviour is near. Oh,
Our watchword is RIGHT and PRESS ONWARD; We dread not the field nor the foe.
How sweetly we'll rest on his bo- som, In Ed - en, dear Eden, our home.

Guide Us, Loving Saviour.

A. W. French. Minnie Minton.

1. Dear and loving Saviour, List- en to our prayer, Take us to thy bosom,
2. Kind and gentle Saviour, Guide us all the way, Keep thy faithful children
3. Hap - py, blessed Saviour, Thine we'll ever be, As we onward journey,

Keep us in thy care; We are youthful pilgrims, Wand'ring here below,
Near thee ev- 'ry day, Lead us in thy footsteps, So we may not roam,
With sweet trust in thee, For we know up yonder, With thee, by and by,

CHORUS.

And we need thee, Jesus, Ev'rywhere we go. Guide us, ev- er guide us,
Till we reach the mansions Of e - ternal home.
We shall live forev - er, In our home on high.

Take us by the hand, Lead us, loving Saviour, To the golden land.

From "Primary Songs," by per.

Fix Your Thoughts on Jesus.

Minnie B. Lowry. J. E. Hall.

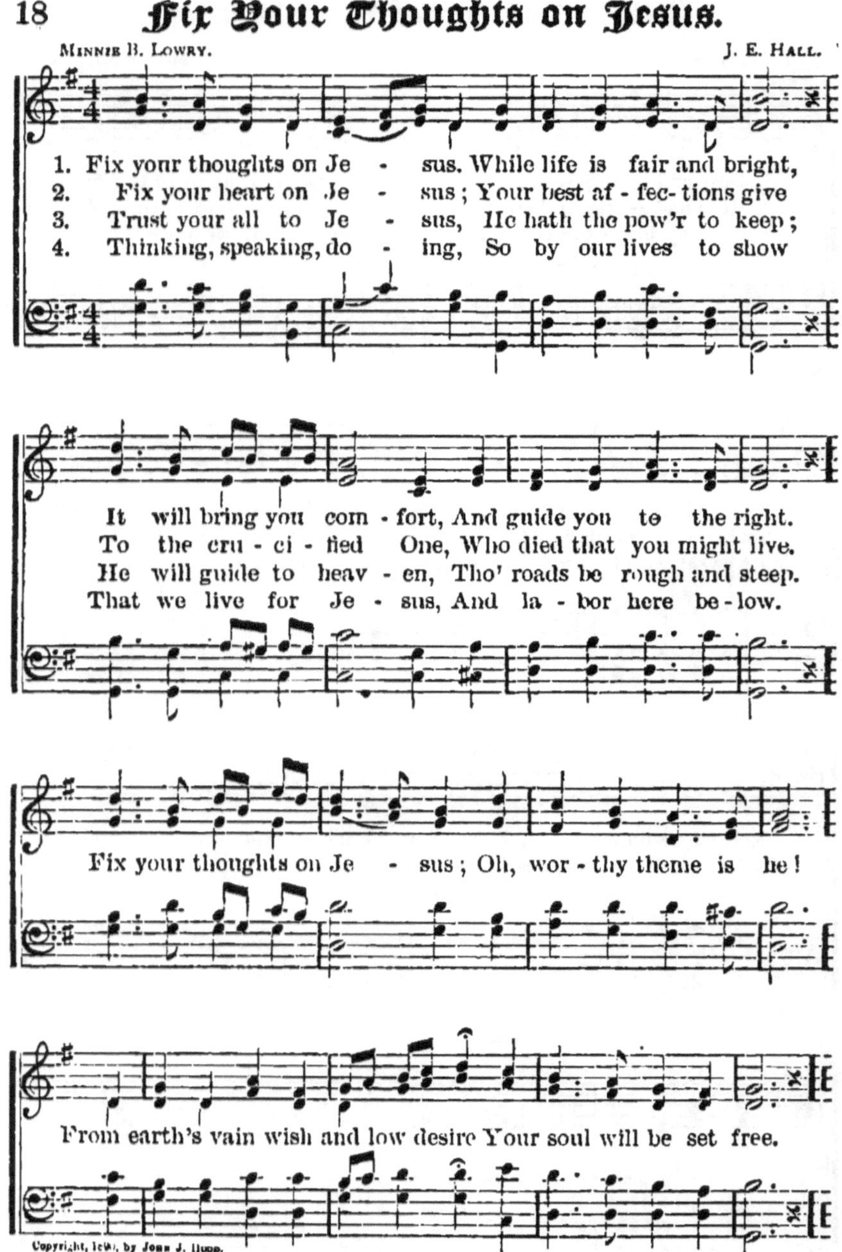
1. Fix your thoughts on Je - sus. While life is fair and bright,
2. Fix your heart on Je - sus; Your best af - fec- tions give
3. Trust your all to Je - sus, He hath the pow'r to keep;
4. Thinking, speaking, do - ing, So by our lives to show
It will bring you com - fort, And guide you to the right.
To the cru - ci - fied One, Who died that you might live.
He will guide to heav - en, Tho' roads be rough and steep.
That we live for Je - sus, And la - bor here be - low.
Fix your thoughts on Je - sus; Oh, wor - thy theme is he!
From earth's vain wish and low desire Your soul will be set free.

O for a Heart Whiter than Snow.

E. E. Hewitt.
Wm. J. Kirkpatrick.
1. O for a heart that is whiter than snow! Kept, ever kept, 'neath the life-giv-ing flow; Cleansed from all pas-sion, self-seeking, and pride, Washed in the fountain of Cal-va-ry's tide.
2. O for a heart that is whiter than snow! Calm in the peace that he loves to be-stow; Dai-ly refreshed by the heav-en-ly dews, Read-y for ser-vice whene'er he shall choose.
3. O for a heart that is whiter than snow! With the pure flame of the Spir-it a-glow; Filled with the love that is true and sin-cere, Love that is a-ble to ban-ish all fear.
4. O for a heart that is whiter than snow! Then in his grace and his knowledge to grow; Grow-ing like him who my pat-tern shall be, Till in his beau-ty my King I shall see.
CHORUS.
O for a heart whit-er than snow! Sa-viour di-vine, to whom else can I go? Thou who didst die, loving me so, Give me a heart that is whiter than snow.
Copyright, 1892, by Wm. J. Kirkpatrick.

We Are Ever Marching On.

F. G. Burroughs. Adam Geibel.

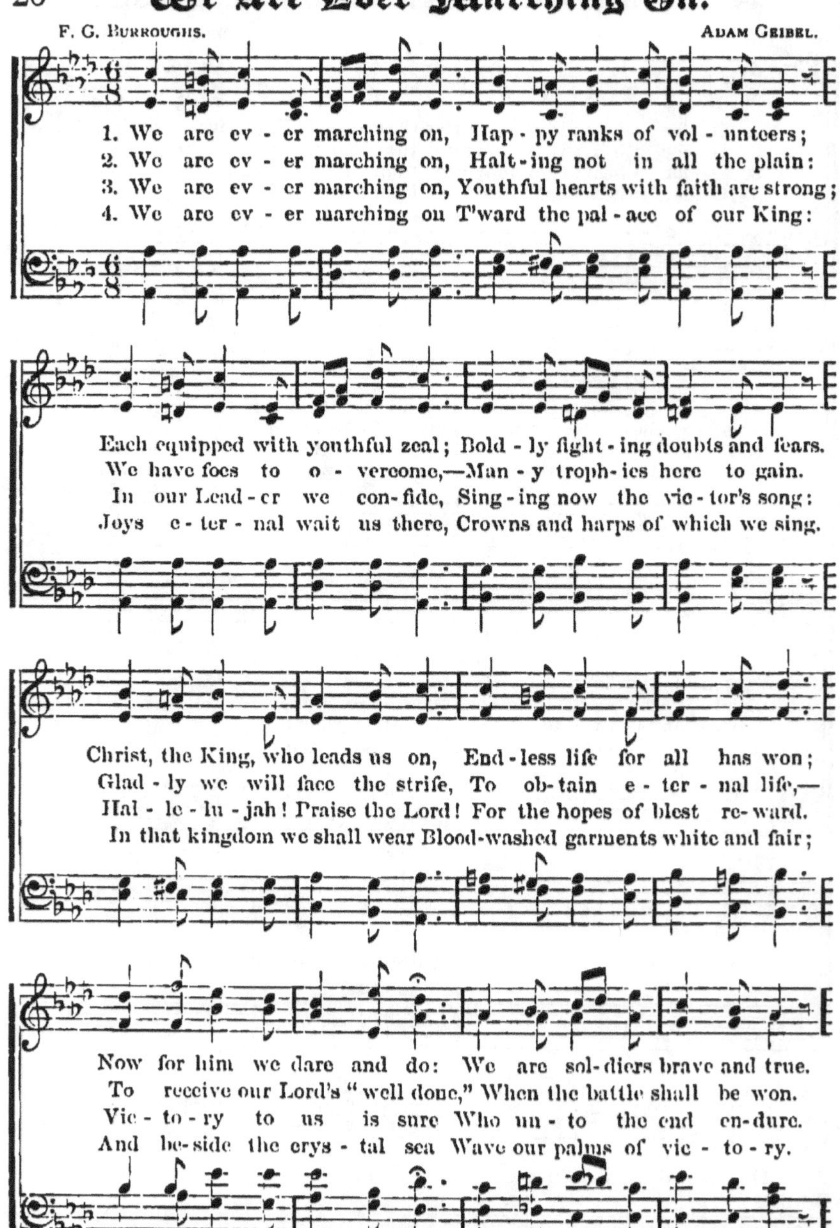
1. We are ev - er marching on, Hap - py ranks of vol - unteers;
2. We are ev - er marching on, Halt - ing not in all the plain:
3. We are ev - er marching on, Youthful hearts with faith are strong;
4. We are ev - er marching on T'ward the pal - ace of our King:
Each equipped with youthful zeal; Bold - ly fight - ing doubts and fears.
We have foes to o - vercome,—Man - y troph - ies here to gain.
In our Lead - er we con - fide, Sing - ing now the vic - tor's song:
Joys e - ter - nal wait us there, Crowns and harps of which we sing.
Christ, the King, who leads us on, End - less life for all has won;
Glad - ly we will face the strife, To ob - tain e - ter - nal life,—
Hal - le - lu - jah! Praise the Lord! For the hopes of blest re - ward.
In that kingdom we shall wear Blood-washed garments white and fair;
Now for him we dare and do: We are sol - diers brave and true.
To receive our Lord's "well done," When the battle shall be won.
Vic - to - ry to us is sure Who un - to the end en - dure.
And be - side the crys - tal sea Wave our palms of vic - to - ry.

Marching to Jerusalem.

E. H. Lide.
Wm. J. Kirkpatrick.
1. We are marching to Je - ru - sa- lem the blessed, And we're singing of its glories on the way; To the ci- ty of our King, Where the angel-voices ring, Where there shines forever one unclouded day.
2. We are marching to Je - ru - sa- lem the blessed, But there's work to do for Je- sus as we go; There are helpful words to say, Sorrow's tears to wipe away, Precious seeds, that to the harvest soon will grow.
3. We are marching to Je-rusalem the blessed, And its light streams down upon the path we tread; For the King who reigns above, Comes beside us in his love, By the banners of his mercy we are led.
CHORUS.
‖: Marching on, :‖ with joyful hosannas, Our songs shall rise on faith's triumphant wing; But we'll sing more sweetly there, In His presence, bright and fair, In Jerusalem, the city of our King. . . . . .
faith's triumphant wing;
the cit - y of our King.

Carry the Light.

E. E. Hewitt.
Adam Geibel.
1. Many in darkness are far astray, Carry the light, carry the light,
2. Let us u - nite in this blest employ, Carry the light, carry the light;
3. Living for Jesus, we'll work and pray, Carry the light, carry the light;
4. Clearer and clearer the dayspring glows, Carry the light, carry the light;
Spreading the beams of the gospel day, Car- ry the beauti - ful light;
Tell the good news of salvation's joy, Car- ry the beauti - ful light.
Walking with him in the shining way, Car- ry the beauti - ful light;
Brighter and brighter the morning grows, Car- ry the beauti - ful light.
Tell them the gift of the Father's love, How the dear Saviour he gave;
Singing of Jesus, our songs are bright, Bright with the blessing he brings;
O, there's a glory that fills the heart, Sunshine of pardon and peace;
Jesus is coming in wondrous might, Coming in splendor to reign;
Tell them of mercy that smiles above, Je- sus, almight- y to save!
Helping to scatter the shades of night. Sing of the Lord's healing wings.
Let us the se- cret to all impart, Helping the kingdom's increase.
Sorrow and sighing shall take their flight, E- den shall blossom a - gain.

Jesus Knows My Name.

F. G. Burroughs.
Jno. R. Sweney.
1. Ma - ry stood be-side the tomb, Ah! her heart was bro - ken;
2. When my heart is sad with fear, And my spir - it bro - ken,
3. When I walk through death's dark vale, Will he then be near me?
Near her was the ris - en Lord, Yet he had not spo - ken:
Will I know him in the dark By the same sweet to - ken?
Will my lov - ing Saviour's voice Whis-per words to cheer me?
But when Je - sus gent - ly came Close to her, and called her name,
Will he put my fears to shame When he kind - ly speaks my name
Yes, he'll know me just the same, He will call me by my name
Hap - py then was Ma - ry, Hap - py then was Ma - ry.
As he spoke to Ma - ry? As he spoke to Ma - ry?
As he then called Ma - ry, As he then called Ma - ry.

Stepping in the Light.

L. H. Edmunds. W. J. Kirkpatrick.

1. Trying to walk in the steps of the Saviour, Trying to follow our Saviour and King; Shaping our lives by his blessed ex-am-ple, Happy, how happy, the songs that we bring.
2. Pressing more closely to him who is leading, When we are tempted to turn from the way; Trusting the arm that is strong to defend us, Happy, how happy, our praises each day.
3. Walking in footsteps of gen-tle forbearance, Footsteps of faithfulness, mer-cy, and love, Looking to him for the grace free-ly promised, Happy, how happy, our journey above.
4. Trying to walk in the steps of the Saviour, Upward, still upward we'll fol-low our Guide, When we shall see him, "the King in his beauty," Happy, how happy, our place at his side.

CHORUS.

How beautiful to walk in the steps of the Saviour, Stepping in the light, Stepping in the light; How beautiful to walk in the steps of the Saviour, Led in paths of light.

The Child of a King.

HATTIE E. BUELL.
Arr. from Melody by Rev. JOHN B. SUMNER.
1. My Father is rich in houses and lands, He holdeth the wealth of the world in his hands! Of rubies and diamonds, of sil - ver and gold His cof- fers are full,—he has riches untold.
2. My Father's own Son, the Saviour from sin, Once wander'd o'er earth as the poorest of men, But now he is reigning for- ev - er on high, And will give me a home in heaven by and by.
3. I once was an outcast stranger on earth, A sinner by choice, an al - ien by birth! But I've been adopted, my name's written down,—An heir to a mansion, a robe and a crown.
4. A tent or a cottage, why should I care? They're building a palace for me o - ver there! Tho' exiled from home, yet, still I may sing: All glo - ry to God, I'm the child of a King.
CHORUS.
I'm the child of a King, The child of a King; With Je - sus my Saviour I'm the child of a King.
ad lib.

Joyfully, Joyfully.

Mrs. Sharpless. "We rejoice in hope of the glory of God."—Rom. v. 2. Wm. J. Kirkpatrick.

1. Oh, joy-ful-ly, joy-ful-ly, onward we go; We see not our path, but our
2. Though trials as-sail us, and dangers affright, And nearer, still nearer, comes
3. Then onward, still onward, thro' life's varied track, In hope we press on, nor look
Lead-er we know; And where'er he may guide us, thro' shadow or sun.
death's aw-ful night; Yet what shall dis-may us, when close at our side,
mournful-ly back; With our Saviour be-side us to point out our way,
CHORUS.
Ev-er joy-ful-ly, joy-ful-ly fol-low we on. Joy-ful-ly, joy-ful-ly,
Stands he who can help us, our Saviour and Guide.
We'll joy-ful-ly speed us thro' life's little day.
forward we go, Joy-ful-ly leav-ing all sor-row be-low; Onward and
upward, tho' Sa-tan as-sail; Joy-ful-ly onward, thro' Christ we'll prevail.

Happy Tidings.

Lizzie Edwards. Jno. R. Sweney.

1. Tidings, happy tidings, Hark! hark! the sound! Hear the joyful ech- o
2. Tidings, happy tidings, Hark! hark! they say, Do not slight the warning,
3. Tidings, happy tidings, Hark! hark! a- gain! Rushing o'er the mountain,
Thro' the world resound; Christ the Lord proclaims them, Hear and heed the call,
Come, oh, come to-day; Christ, our loving Saviour, Still repeats the call,
Sweeping o'er the plain; Onward goes the message, 'Tis the Saviour's call,
REFRAIN.
Come, ye starving ones that perish, Room, room for all. Whosoev - er asketh,
Come, ye weary, heavy - laden, Room, room for all.
Come, for ev'rything is ready, Room, room for all.
Jesus will receive; Whosoever thirsteth, Jesus will relieve; See the living

For Christ and the Church.

E. E. Hewitt.
Wm. J. Kirkpatrick.
1. For Christ and the church, let our voi-ces ring, Let us hon - or the
2. For Christ and the church, be our earnest prayer, Let us fol - low his
3. For Christ and the church, willing off'rings make. Time and talents and
4. For Christ and the church, let us cast a - side, By his con - quering
name of our own blessed King, Let us work with a will in the
ban - ner, the cross dai - ly bear, Let us yield, wholly yield, to his
gold, for the dear Master's sake; We'll re - member the best we can
grace, chains of self, fear, and pride; May our lives be enriched by an
strength of youth, And loy - al - ly stand for the kingdom of truth.
Spir - it's power, And faithful - ly serve him in life's brightest hour.
bring to him, The heart's wealth of love, that will nev- er grow dim.
aim so grand, Then hap - py the call to the Saviour's right hand.
CHORUS.
For Christ our dear Redeem - er, For Christ who died to save,
For the Church his blood hath purchased, Lord, make us pure and brave.

A little Talk with Jesus.

Wm. G. Fischer.

1. A lit - tle talk with Je - sus, How it smooths the rugged road!
2. Ah, this is what I'm wanting, His love - ly face to see;
3. I can - not live without him, Nor would I if I could;
4. So I'll wait a lit - tle long - er, Till his appoint - ed time,
How it seems to help me on- ward, When I faint beneath my load;
And I'm not a- fraid to say it, I know he's wanting me.
He is my dai - ly por - tion, My med - i - cine and food.
And a- long the upward path- way My pil - grim feet shall climb.
When my heart is crushed with sorrow, And my eyes with tears are dim,
He gave his life a ran - som, To make me all his own,
He is al - to- geth - er love - ly; None can with him com - pare;
There, in my Father's dwell- ing, Where man - y mansions be,
There is naught can yield me comfort Like a lit - tle talk with him.
And he'll ne'er forget his prom - ise To me, his purchased one.
Chief - est among ten thousand, And fair - est of the fair.
I shall sweetly talk with Je - sus, And he will talk with me.

By permission.

Rally for the Right.

Rev. E. A. Hoffman. | Wm. J. Kirkpatrick.

1. Sol-diers recruiting in the ranks of the Lord, Fall in - to line,
2. There is a bat-tle to be fought in the right, Fall in - to line,
3. Earnest the conflict, needing brave men and strong, Fall in - to line,

fall in - to line; Gird on the ar-mor, both the shield and the sword,
fall in - to line; And we can win it if we strike in our might,
fall in - to line; We will not falt-er though the struggle be long,

Fall in - to line, fall in - to line.

CHORUS.

Ral-ly, then; ral-ly, then; ral-ly for the right; God needs the brave and true;

God needs the true, Then

Ral-ly, then; rally, then; ral-ly in your might; God is call-ing you.

Put Your Trust in God.

E. A. Barnes.
Jno. R. Sweney.
1. Trust God as a child of his love, Trust in him to guide you with his eye;
2. Trust God when the tempter is near, Trust in him for grace to turn aside;
3. Trust God at the coming of grief, Trust in him to soothe its bitter pain:
4. Trust God as you journey a- long, Trust in him for grace to win the prize;
Trust God for the blessings of life, And which he will sup- ply.
Trust God 'mid the billows of life A ref - uge to provide.
Trust God 'mid the burdens of life To strengthen and sustain.
Trust God till you answer the call To meet him in the skies.
CHORUS.
Trust God as he has told you, And look to him from day to day;
Put your trust in God, Put your trust in God As the guardian of your way.

Children of the Kingdom.

Fanny J. Crosby.
Jno. R. Sweney
1. Chil-dren of the king-dom, while we jour-ney here, On - ly for a
2. Chil-dren of the king-dom, press-ing on our way, Nev - er let us
3. Chil-dren of the king-dom, while we watch and wait, Nev - er be dis-
4. Chil-dren of the king-dom, joy - ful let us be, Yon - der is the
time a - bid - ing; Looking un - to Je - sus, ban - ish ev' - ry fear,
fal - ter, nev - er; Bear the cross for Je - sus, bear it ev' - ry day,
cour-aged, nev - er; Soon our feet will en - ter thro' the pal - ace gate,
shin - ing riv - er; There in all his beau - ty we the King shall see,
D.S.—Children of the kingdom, tar - ry not, but come
Fine. CHORUS.
For his eyes our path is guid - ing. From the land of song, the
In his mer - cy trust-ing ev - er.
And go out no more for - ev - er.
And be-hold his face for - ev - er.
Where the pure in heart are call - ing.
D.S.
bright land of song, List - en to the mu - sic gent - ly fall - ing;

C. S. Broom. — E. D. Beale.

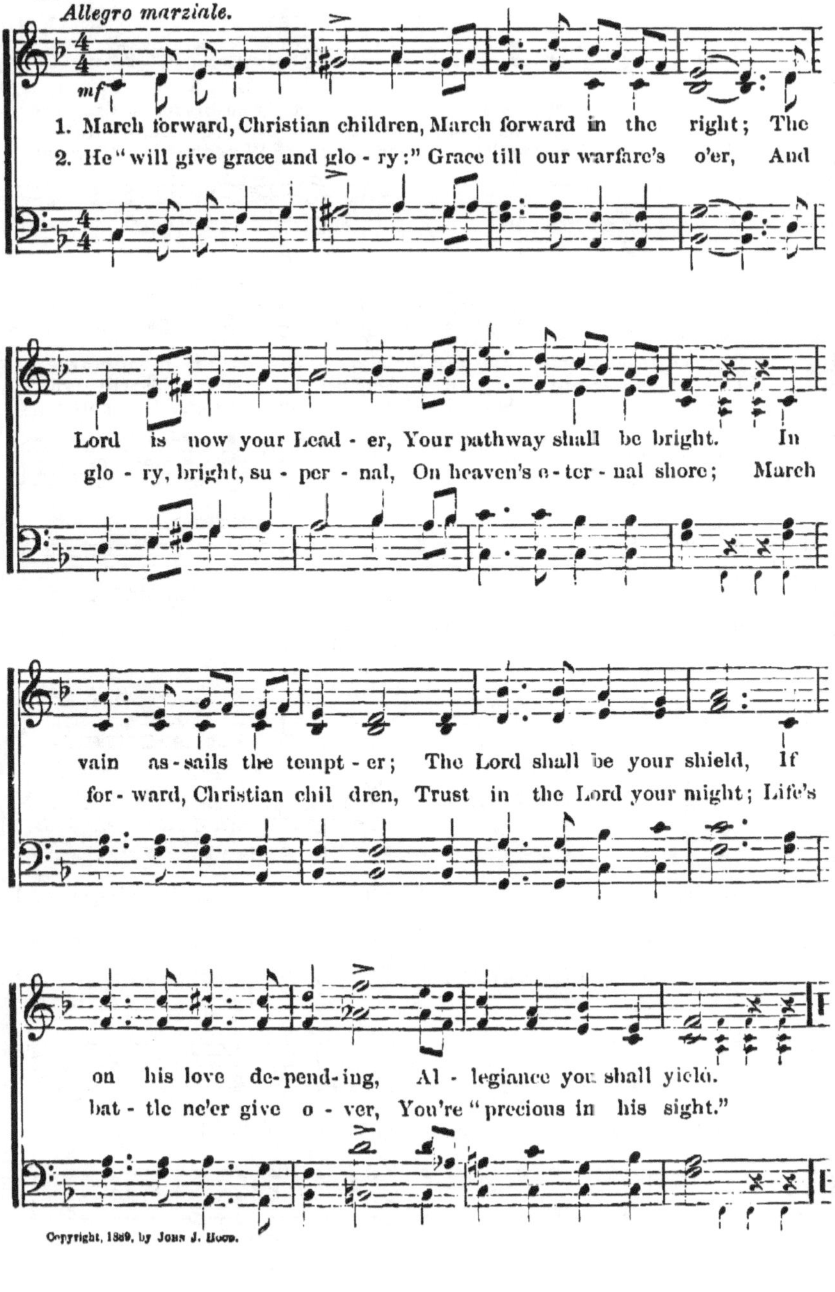

Allegro marziale.

mf

1. March forward, Christian children, March forward in the right; The
2. He "will give grace and glo - ry:" Grace till our warfare's o'er, And

Lord is now your Lead - er, Your pathway shall be bright. In
glo - ry, bright, su - per - nal, On heaven's e - ter - nal shore; March

vain as - sails the tempt - er; The Lord shall be your shield, If
for - ward, Christian chil dren, Trust in the Lord your might; Life's

on his love de - pend - ing, Al - legiance you shall yield.
bat - tle ne'er give o - ver, You're "precious in his sight."

Comrades in Endeavor.

E. E. Hewitt. Jno. R. Sweney.

1. Ask the gracious Master For a willing heart, From his blessed service
2. Faithful in the lit- tle, Looking ev- 'ry day For the simple duties
3. He who works for Jesus, "Faithful in the least," Wins the blest approval
Nev - er to depart; Faithful he who calls us, Ev- 'ry promise true,
Ly - ing in our way; Little words of comfort Loving lips will speak,
At the heav'nly feast; So we'll ask this blessing, His enabling power,
Strengthened by his Spirit We'll be faithful too.
Little acts of kindness Willing hearts will seek.
Hearti - ly to serve him Ev- 'ry day and hour.
CHORUS.
Comrades in Endeavor,
ready, ready! Faithful, true and faithful, may we ever be; Marching, onward
marching, steady, steady! Comrades of the Junior Y. P. S. C. E.
Copyright, 1892, by Jno. R. Sweney.

Sing the New Song.

EMMA PITT. ADAM GEIBEL.

1. Children of Zi - on, sing the new song, Praises to Je- sus in
2. Christ our Redeemer, Saviour and Friend, Points to a home where
3. Children of promise, heirs to a King, Loud let ho- san - nas
gladness prolong; Him that hath loved us, praise with the voice, Washed from our
joys never end; Here on the earth is conflict and woe, Sing with the
gratefully ring; Paid is the ransom bought with his blood, Songs of re-
CHORUS.
sins, in freedom re - joice. Beauti - ful songs, beauti- ful
heart as onward we go.
demption sing un- to God.
songs, Sung by the an - gels in heaven a - bove; Beau- ti - ful
songs, beautiful songs, Beautiful songs of redeeming love.
Copyright, 1892, by John J. Hood.

O, Work for the Master.

L. H. Edmunds. Jno. R. Sweney

1 O, work for the Mas - ter; the field is so wide, Wherev - er God
2. Yes, work for the Mas - ter; at home, by the way, You meet precious
3. Sweet work for the Mas - ter! you toil not a - lone, Your weakness and
puts you in pa - tience a - bide; Be faith - ful in lit - tle, for
souls, for whom la - bor and pray; "The Lord giv- eth wis- dom," he'll
needs to your Sa - viour are known; He'll strengthen and help you, while
then you shall know How much greater blessing the Lord can be- stow.
give it to you, If ear - nest - ly ask - ing," Lord, what shall I do."
life pass - es by, Then give you a share in his triumph on high.
CHORUS.
Do something for Je - sus! Do something for Je - sus! "Go, work in my
rit. a tempo.
vineyard," O hear him now say, Do something for Je - sus! Do

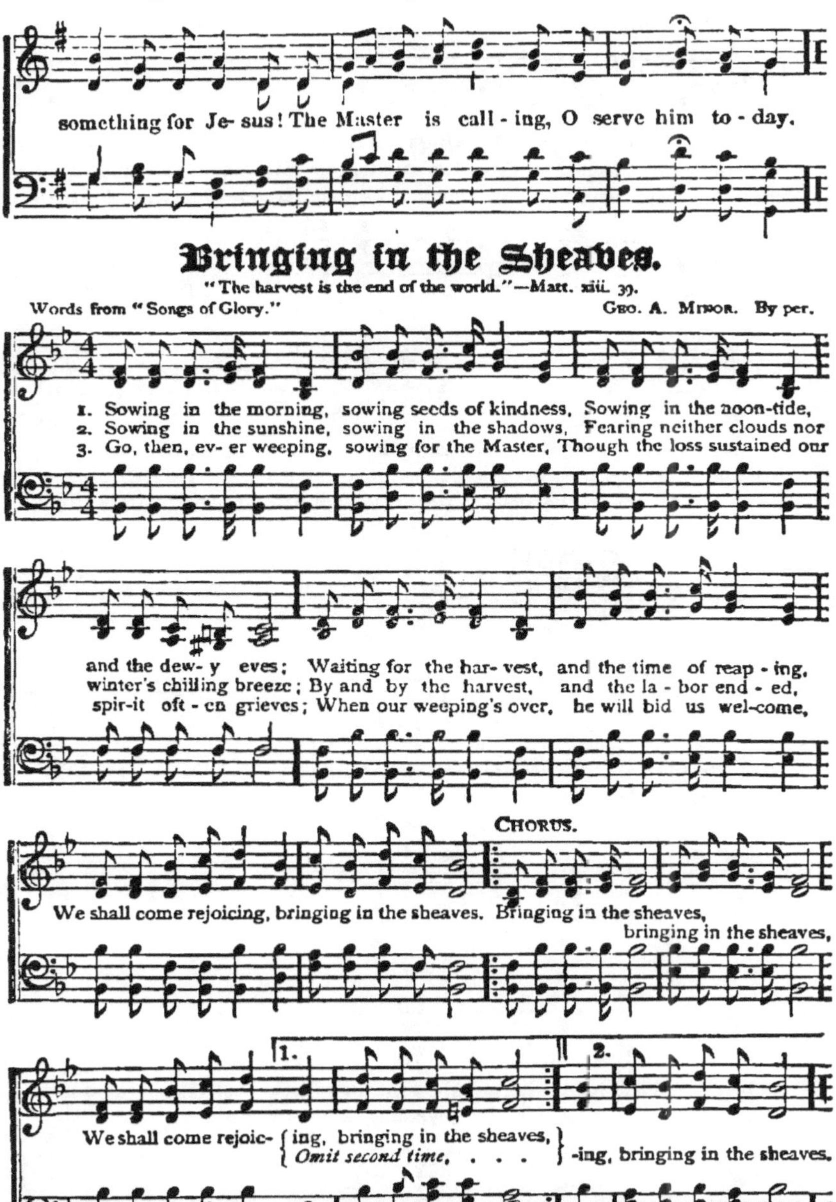
something for Je- sus! The Master is call - ing, O serve him to - day.
Bringing in the Sheaves.
"The harvest is the end of the world."—Matt. xiii. 39.
Words from "Songs of Glory."
Geo. A. Minor. By per.
1. Sowing in the morning, sowing seeds of kindness, Sowing in the noon-tide,
2. Sowing in the sunshine, sowing in the shadows, Fearing neither clouds nor
3. Go, then, ev- er weeping, sowing for the Master, Though the loss sustained our
and the dew- y eves; Waiting for the har- vest, and the time of reap - ing,
winter's chilling breeze; By and by the harvest, and the la - bor end - ed,
spir-it oft - en grieves; When our weeping's over, he will bid us wel-come,
Chorus.
We shall come rejoicing, bringing in the sheaves. Bringing in the sheaves,
bringing in the sheaves,
1.
2.
We shall come rejoic- ing, bringing in the sheaves,
Omit second time, . . .
-ing, bringing in the sheaves.

Joy Bells.

MARTHA J. LANKTON.
WM. J. KIRKPATRICK.
1. Pretty, golden sunbeams, Looking from the sky, Call us now to wake and sing
2. Pretty birds that carol From the waving trees, Hiding in the branches green,
3. Shall our tongues be silent? Have we naught to say, When our hearts can feel his love
Praise to God on high; Song and beauty ev'rywhere, On the earth and in the air,
Cradled on the breeze, Thro' the laughing summer days Still their great Creator praise;
Better far than they? Like the beams that sparkle bright, Like the birds on pinions light,
CHORUS.
Still the blessed truth declare, God, our God, is love. Joy bells, joy bells,
In the simple tones they raise Telling God is love.
Like the bells, let all u-nite, Singing, God is love. Joy bells, joy bells, merry joy bells,
Repeat pp.
Hear them ringing, sweetly ringing; Hear the joy bells, joy bells Echo God is love.
joy bells, joy bells, merry joy bells
Copyright, 1886, by John J. Hood.

His Child I want to be.

Rev. C. H. Yatman. Jno. R. Sweney.

1. The children to Je-sus may come And life and sal-va-tion re-ceive;
2. My name will he write in his book, And call me a lamb of his fold;
3. I read in his own blessed word How lit-tle ones use-ful may be.
New hearts will he give ev-'ry one, If on him they on-ly be-lieve.
When Satan shall seek to devour, Then me in his hands will he hold.
I'll stand with my face to the cross, That oth-ers the Saviour may see.
CHORUS.
I will love him, I will love him, For his child I want to be;
On the cross he died for sin-ners, On the cross he died for me.

The Everlasting Hymn.

E. E. Hewitt.
B. Hillyard Sweney.
1. Ho - ly, ho - ly, ho - ly; An - gel voi - ces sing - ing;
2. Ho - ly, ho - ly, ho - ly; Grandest mu - sic swell - ing;
3. Ho - ly, ho - ly, ho - ly; Come, let us a - dore him;
Ho - ly, ho - ly, ho - ly, Thro' high heav - en ring - ing.
Ho - ly, ho - ly, ho - ly, All sweet notes ex - cell - ing.
Ho - ly, ho - ly, ho - ly, Hum - bly bow be - fore him.
From that temple, pure and bright, Bathed in streams of crystal light,
Those who conquered by his might, Wearing now their crowns of light,
Wisdom, glo - ry, love and might, With the ser - a - phim u - nite
Hear the ev - er - lasting hymn, Ho - ly, ho - ly, ho - ly.
Join the ev - er - lasting hymn, Ho - ly, ho - ly, ho - ly.
In the ev - er - lasting hymn, Ho - ly, ho - ly, ho - ly.

Happy Days.

E. E. Hewitt. Jno R. Sweney.

1. On - ly to follow, day by day, Just as the Master leads the way,
2. On - ly his least command to heed, Letting his fulness meet our need;
3. On - ly to trust him all the while, Trusting, while days of pleasure smile,
4. On - ly in Je - sus to a - bide, Cleansing the soul in Calv'ry's tide,
Taking each step that leads above In the bright sunshine of his love.
Loy - al to him thro' good and ill, Finding his grace suf- ficient still.
Trusting, when tears of sorrow fall, Proving his presence, more than all.
On - ly to praise him more and more, Till face to face, on Eden's shore.
CHORUS.
Happy days, yes, happy days; Faithful in service, joyful with praise;
Happy days, yes, happy days, Walking with Jesus in his ways.

Ring Out the Hallelujahs.

MISS EMMA M. JOHNSTON. WM. J. KIRKPATRICK.

1. Sing the song the ransomed sing, Let your hal- le - lujahs ring,
2. Sing the love that set you free; Sing the song of lib - er - ty,
3. Sing the grace that made you whole; Sing the vict'ries of the soul,
4. Sing till heaven shall catch the strain, Hallelu - jah yet a - gain,

Glo - ry to the Lord your King; Ring out the halle - lujahs.
Sing the glo - ry yet to be; Ring out the hal - le - lujahs.
Sing while time shall onward roll; Ring out the hal - le - lujahs.
"Love redeeming" the refrain; Ring out the hal - le - lujahs.

REFRAIN.

Hal - le - lu - jah! . . . . Hal - le - lu - jah! . . . .
Hal - le - lu - jah! Hal - le - lu - jah!

Glo ry to our Lord and King; Ring out the halle - lu- jahs.

O Christian, Awake!

"Stand, therefore, having your loins girt about with truth, and having on the breastplate of righteousness."

Arr. from "Singing Pilgrim."

1. O Christian, a- wake! for the strife is at hand, With helmet and shield
2. Whatev- er thy danger, take heed and beware, And turn not thy back,
3. The cause of thy Master with vig- or defend; O watch, fight, and pray—
4. Press on, nev- er doubting; thy Captain is near, With grace to supply,

and a sword in thy hand; To meet the bold tempter go, fearless- ly go,
for no ar- mor is there; The legions of darkness if thou would'st o'erthrow,
persevere to the end; Wherev- er he leads thee go, valiant- ly go,
and with comfort to cheer; His love, like a stream, in the desert will flow,

And stand like the brave, with thy face to the foe.
Then stand like the brave, with thy face to the foe.
And stand like the brave, with thy face to the foe.
Then stand like the brave, with thy face to the foe.

REFRAIN.

Stand like the brave, Stand like the brave,

Stand like the brave, Stand like the brave, Stand like the brave, with thy face to the foe.

The Land Immortal.

E. E. Hewitt. Florence W. Williams.

1. Yonder beams the land immor - tal, Rich in glo - ries still untold;
2. Ma - ny-jew - eled its foundations, Rainbow-tint - ed are its walls;
3. Shall we view that cit - y golden? Like a crys - tal glowing clear,
Gleams with pearl each shining por - tal, All its streets of pur - est gold.
Hear the songs of ju - bi - la - tion Ringing thro' its pal - ace-halls.
Where no joy is e'er withhold- en, Where there's never pain nor fear.
Words can ne'er the beau- ty ren - der Of this cit - y fair and bright,
O, to join those anthems peal- ing, With the white-robed throng unite,
If we love and serve the Sa- viour, Wholly trust his saving might,
Radiant with e - ternal splendor, For the Lamb shall be its light.
Where the Lamb, his face re - veal- ing. Is the ev - er - lasting light.
We shall meet to praise for- ev - er, Where the Lamb shall be our light.

Fruitful Branches.

E. E. Hewitt. Jno. R. Sweney.

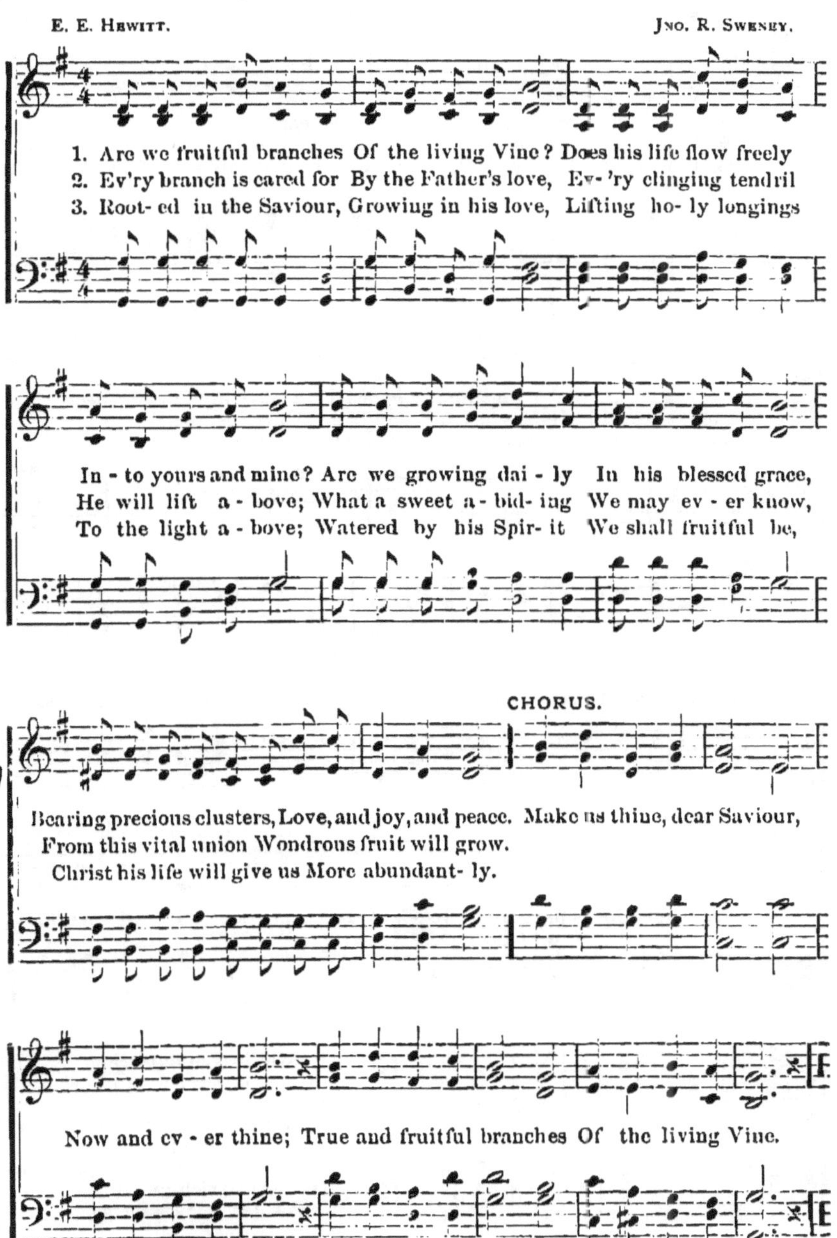
1. Are we fruitful branches Of the living Vine? Does his life flow freely
2. Ev'ry branch is cared for By the Father's love, Ev- 'ry clinging tendril
3. Root- ed in the Saviour, Growing in his love, Lifting ho- ly longings
In - to yours and mine? Are we growing dai - ly In his blessed grace,
He will lift a - bove; What a sweet a - bid- ing We may ev - er know,
To the light a - bove; Watered by his Spir- it We shall fruitful be,
Bearing precious clusters, Love, and joy, and peace.
From this vital union Wondrous fruit will grow.
Christ his life will give us More abundant- ly.
CHORUS.
Make us thine, dear Saviour,
Now and ev - er thine; True and fruitful branches Of the living Vine.

Jesus Loves Me so.

W. H. Flaville. (From "The Wells of Salvation," by per.) Jno. R. Swenby.

1. I love my Saviour dear,—How much can never tell; He comes so
2. I love his own dear word, The book of books to me, In ev-'ry
3. I love his ho-ly day, The day he calls his own, That keeps me
ver-y near, And with him all is well; I love my Saviour dear, How
land is heard Its gos-pel full and free. I love his own dear word, With
on the way To my ce-les-tial home, I love his ho-ly day, That
much can never show; He makes my pathway clear, And ever loves me so.
love 'tis all a-glow, My very heart is stirr'd, For Je-sus loves me so.
gives me grace to grow, And ever watch and pray, For Jesus loves me so.
CHORUS.
Je-sus loves me so, Je-sus loves me so, I will love him
more and more, For Jesus loves me so.

4 I love the Sunday-school,
Oh, who can stay away?
Its teachings be my rule
Of life from day to day,
I love the Sunday-school;
Oh, would that all might know
Its joys so rich and full,
For Jesus loves me so.

Blessed Assurance.

F. J. CROSBY. "He is faithful that hath promised."—Heb. x. 23. Mrs. JOS. F. KNAPP.

1. Blessed as - surance, Jesus is mine! Oh, what a foretaste of glory di - vine! Heir of sal - va - tion, purchase of God, Born of his Spir - it, washed in his blood.
2. Perfect sub-mis-sion, perfect de - light, Visions of rap - ture burst on my sight, Angels descend - ing, bring from a - bove Echoes of mer - cy, whispers of love.
3. Perfect sub-mis-sion, all is at rest, I in my Saviour am happy and blest, Watching and waiting, looking a - bove, Filled with his goodness, lost in his love.
CHORUS.
This is my sto - ry, this is my song, Praising my Sav - iour all the day long; This is my sto - ry, this is my song, Praising my Saviour all the day long.

Marching with Gladness.

S. MARTIN. M. D. KIRKPATRICK.

1. Marching with gladness on our way, Looking to Jesus day by day, Trying his
2. Marching with gladness, joy, and song, Telling of Jesus all day long, Trying the
3. Marching in pastures green and fair, Jesus our Saviour leads us there, Marching by
wondrous love to show, we onward go; Marching with gladness, naught to fear,
precious seed to sow, we onward go; Marching with courage, brave and true,
cooling streams that flow, we onward go; Marching together, oh, how sweet
Jesus our Saviour still is near, Sweeter, oh, sweet - er than music his
Keeping the Saviour still in view, Asking each mo - ment for wisdom and
Over the river when we meet, Gather with Je - sus for- ev- er, our
name we hear.
strength a-new.
joy complete.
CHORUS.
March - - - ing away, a - way, ...
Marching away, away, We're marching away, away,
March - - - ing from day to day; . . . . Un - - - der his
Marching from day to day, We're marching from day to day; Under his banner, how calm
Copyright, 1892, by Wm. J. Kirkpatrick.

banner, how calm and blest He mak - eth his own to rest. . . . . .
how calm and blest He maketh his own to rest.

Happy in the Lord My Saviour.

HENRIETTA E. BLAIR. WM. J. KIRKPATRICK.

1. Happy in the Lord my Sa - viour, Happy as a heart can be;
2. Happy in the Lord my Sa - viour, Trusting him from hour to hour;
3. Happy in the Lord my Sa - viour, Happy when the skies are bright;
4. Glo-ry to the Lord my Sa - viour, Glo- ry to the Lord my King;

Walking in the light that shin - eth Ev- er like a star for me. *Fine.*
Leaning on his arm of mer - cy, Fearing not the tempter's power.
Happy though the clouds may gather, Happy in the deepest night.
Happy in a full sal - va - tion, Glo- ry to his name I sing.

D.S.—"Blessed are the poor in spir - it," "Blessed are the pure in heart."

CHORUS. *D.S.*

Precious are the words of com - fort, Whispered from the world apart;

Lend a Hand.

J. B. Mackay.
Jno. R. Sweney.
1. Are you sit- ting i - dle, while there's work to do? In the Master's
2. Is your voice now si- lent? there are songs to sing, Help to swell the
3. Do your prayers no lon - ger reach the throne of grace, That some fallen
4. Has your heart ceased yearning precious souls to win? Just a word from
vineyard there's a place for you; Be a faithful servant, ev - er
cho- rus make his prais - es ring; Till the strains are wafted ov - er
brother might his steps re - trace? Every prayer will help him from the
you might rescue one from sin; Work with all the strength you have at
read - y stand, Where the Master calls you, lend a helping hand.
all the land, Reaching up to heav - en, lend a helping hand.
sink - ing sand, Yours to - day may save him, lend a helping hand.
your command, Je - sus will re - ward you, lend a helping hand.
CHORUS.
1st.
Lend a hand, lend a hand, lend a helping hand; Precious ones are falling,
2d.
Lend a helping hand. Je- sus still is calling, Lend a helping hand.
Copyright, 1892, by Jno. R. Sweney.

Like an Army We are Marching.

SALLIE MARTIN. WM. J. KIRKPATRICK.

1. Like an arm - y we are marching, In the service of the Lord;
Marching onward to the vict- 'ry He has promised in his word.

2. Like an arm - y we are marching, With our banners, day by day,
Looking ev - er un - to Je - sus, Trusting him to guide our way.

3. Like an arm - y we are marching, From the Sunday-school we come;
Trained to fol- low our Commander, Till he brings us safe - ly home.

4. Like an arm - y we are marching, Many tri - als tho' we meet,—
We shall count them scores of blessings, When we rest at Jesus' feet.

CHORUS.

March - ing, march - ing, Marching brave and strong, . . .
Marching, marching, we are marching,
Like an arm - y we are march- ing, While we sing our hap- py song.
marching, marching,

The Fountain of Truth.

Ida L. Reed. Wm. J. Kirkpatrick.

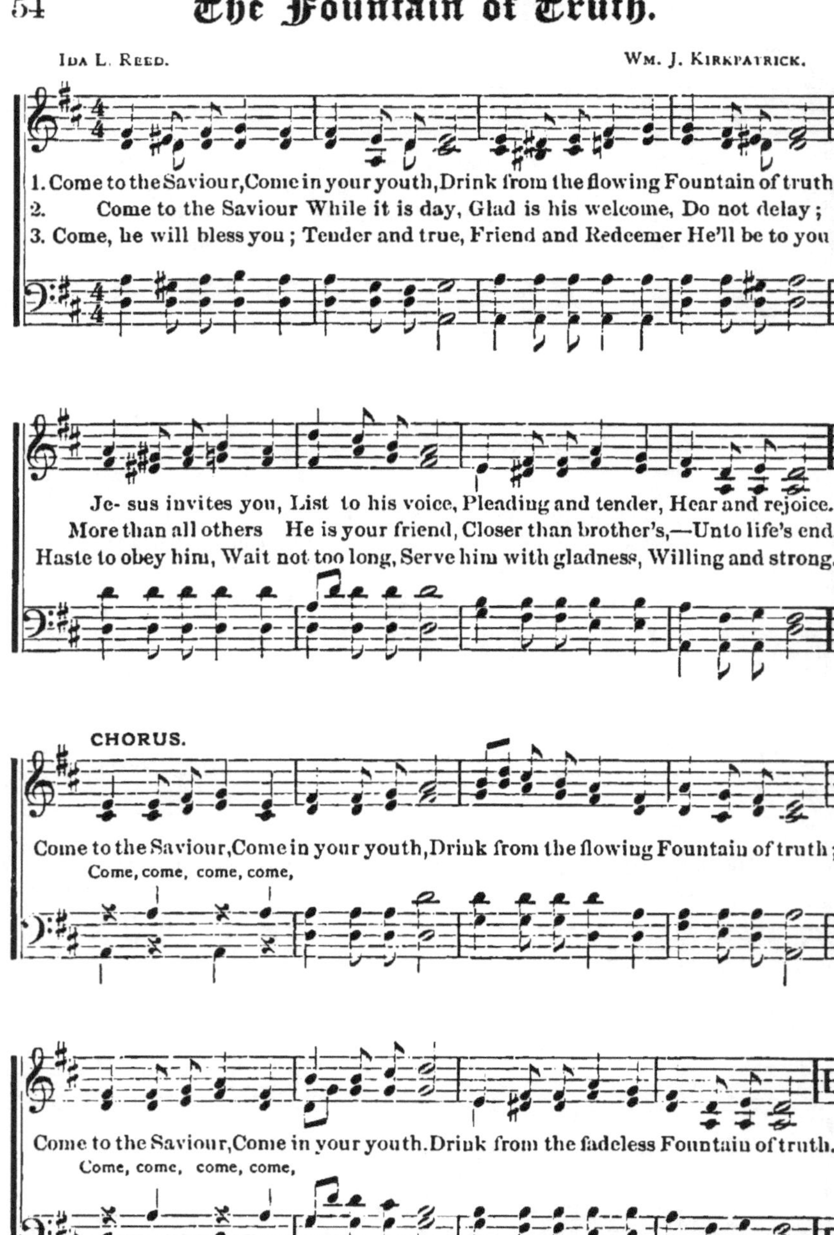
1. Come to the Saviour, Come in your youth, Drink from the flowing Fountain of truth;
2. Come to the Saviour While it is day, Glad is his welcome, Do not delay;
3. Come, he will bless you; Tender and true, Friend and Redeemer He'll be to you;
Je- sus invites you, List to his voice, Pleading and tender, Hear and rejoice.
More than all others He is your friend, Closer than brother's,—Unto life's end.
Haste to obey him, Wait not too long, Serve him with gladness, Willing and strong.
CHORUS.
Come to the Saviour, Come in your youth, Drink from the flowing Fountain of truth;
Come, come, come, come,
Come to the Saviour, Come in your youth. Drink from the fadeless Fountain of truth.
Come, come, come, come,

Go Quickly.

F. G. Burroughs. "The King's business requireth haste."—1 Sam. 21 : 8. Adam Gribel.
1. Go quickly, go, the an-gel - ic words repeating, "Je - sus, the Saviour, liv - eth to-day!" Haste with the news, for the hours of day are fleeting, Oh, tar - ry not by the way.
2. Go quickly, go, ma - ny precious souls are dying, Languishing dai - ly in ways of sin; Hast - en, the words of e - ter - nal freedom cry-ing, Till life and light enter in.
3. Go quickly, join ye the loy - al ranks, obey - ing;—Lovers of Je - sus will not re-fuse: Lose not the smile of your Father by delay - ing; Speed with the bles - sed news.
4. Go quickly, (though many still are unbelieving,) While for the truth in darkness they pine; Pa - tient - ly toil till, their hungry souls reliev-ing, You win the meed di - vine.
Fine.
CHORUS.
Go quickly, in the ear - ly morning; Go quickly, ere it be too late: Go, tell the weary the "better day" is dawning,
D.S.—Where they in dark - ness wait.
D.S.

Coming To-day.

FANNY J. CROSBY. JNO. R. SWENEY.

1. Out on the des-ert, looking, looking, Sinner, 'tis Je-sus looking for thee;
2. Still he is waiting, waiting, waiting, O, what compassion beams in his eye,
3. Lovingly pleading, pleading, pleading, Mercy, tho' slighted, bears with thee yet;
4. Spirits in glory, watching, watching, Long to behold thee safe in the fold;
Tender - ly calling, calling, calling, Hither, thou lost one, O, come unto me.
Hear him repeat-ing gent-ly, gently, Come to thy Saviour, O, why wilt thou die.
Thou canst be happy, hap-py, hap-py, Come, ere thy life-star forever shall set.
Angels are waiting, waiting, waiting, When shall thy story with rapture be told?
CHORUS.
Jesus is looking, Jesus is calling, Why dost thou linger, why tarry away?
Run to him quickly, say to him gladly, Lord, I am coming, coming to-day.
Copyright, 1880, by John J. Hood.

Lay my Sins on Jesus.

Wm. J. Kirkpatrick.

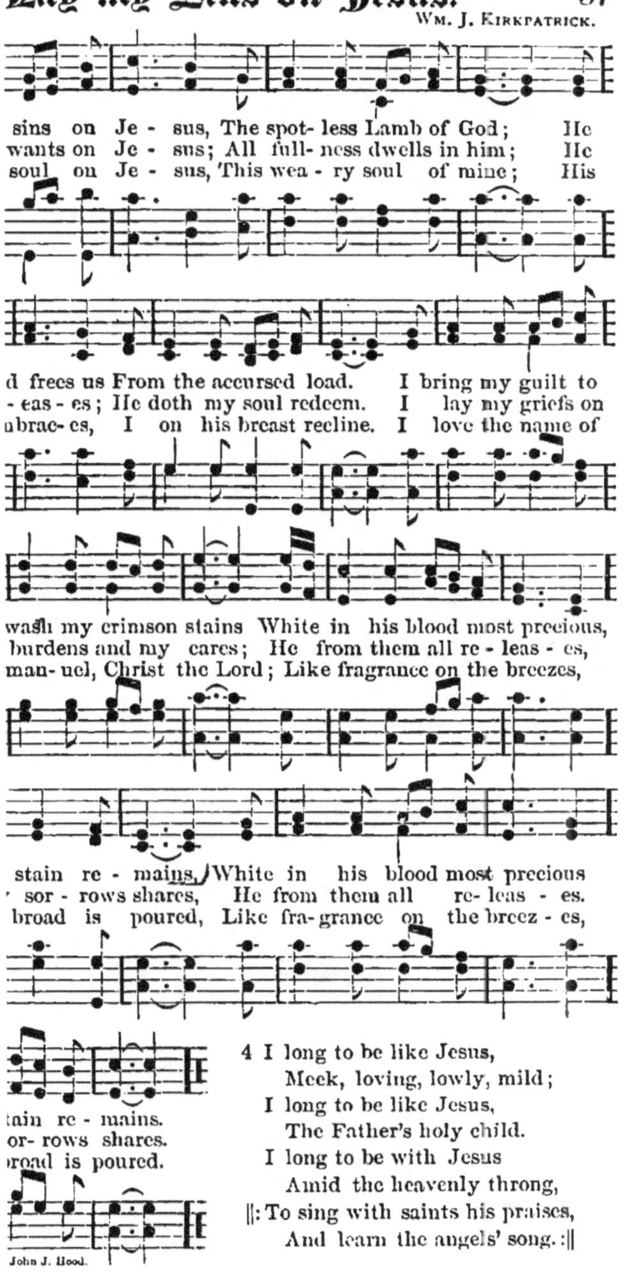
sins on Je - sus, The spot- less Lamb of God; He
wants on Je - sus; All full- ness dwells in him; He
soul on Je - sus, This wea - ry soul of mine; His
d frees us From the accursed load. I bring my guilt to
- eas - es; He doth my soul redeem. I lay my griefs on
nbrac- es, I on his breast recline. I love the name of
wash my crimson stains White in his blood most precious,
burdens and my cares; He from them all re - leas - es,
man- uel, Christ the Lord; Like fragrance on the breezes,
stain re - mains, White in his blood most precious
' sor - rows shares, He from them all re- leas - es.
broad is poured, Like fra- grance on the breez - es,
tain re - mains.
or- rows shares.
road is poured.
John J. Hood.

4 I long to be like Jesus,
Meek, loving, lowly, mild;
I long to be like Jesus,
The Father's holy child.
I long to be with Jesus
Amid the heavenly throng,
‖: To sing with saints his praises,
And learn the angels' song. :‖

Calling You and Me.

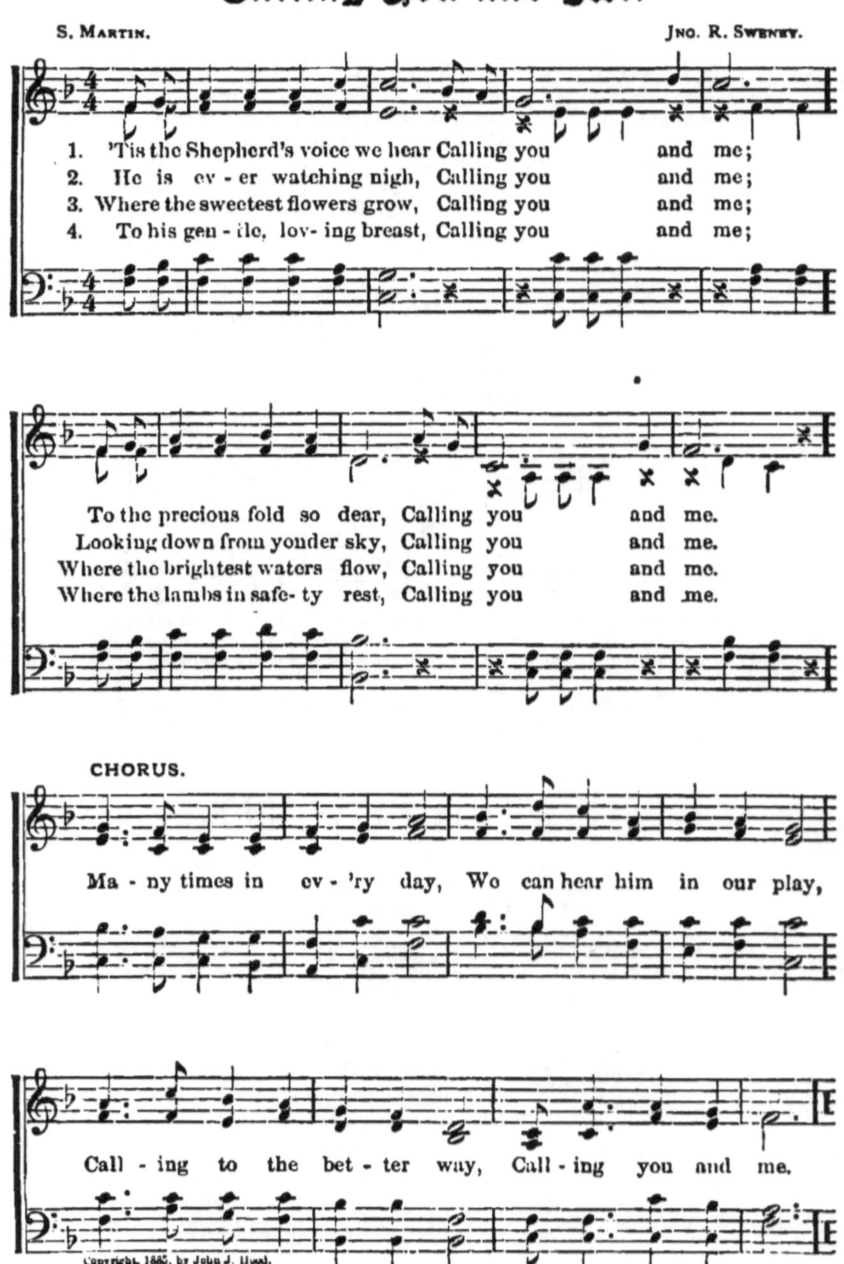
S. Martin.
Jno. R. Sweney.
1. 'Tis the Shepherd's voice we hear Calling you and me;
2. He is ev - er watching nigh, Calling you and me;
3. Where the sweetest flowers grow, Calling you and me;
4. To his gen - tle, lov- ing breast, Calling you and me;
To the precious fold so dear, Calling you and me.
Looking down from yonder sky, Calling you and me.
Where the brightest waters flow, Calling you and me.
Where the lambs in safe- ty rest, Calling you and me.
CHORUS.
Ma - ny times in ev - 'ry day, We can hear him in our play,
Call - ing to the bet - ter way, Call - ing you and me.
Copyright, 1885, by John J. Hood.

Work for Great and Small.

C. S. Boyd.
Adam Geibel.
1. What can we do for Je - sus? Are lit- tle hands so small That they must wait in i - dleness, And do no work at all? The Master who has called us Has, surely, need for all; The Saviour who has bought us Has
2. The golden grain is bending, No reapers come this way, And must the harvest then be lost For lack of them to - day? The Master of the harvest Has, surely, need for all; The Saviour who has bought us Has
3. And in the sun- ny vineyard The purple clusters lie Untouched, be- cause the i - dle ones Are on- ly passing by; The Master of the vineyard Has, surely, need for all; The Saviour who has bought us Has
4. Then let us work for Je - sus, His field is ve - ry wide, And for those who love to serve him He will a way pro - vide; The Master who has called us Has, surely, need for all; The Saviour who has bought us Has
work for great and small;
The Saviour who has bought us
Has work for great and small.

Hosanna in the Highest.

E. E. Hewitt.
Wm. J. Kirkpatrick.
1. In the beautiful temple the children sang
2. To the beautiful temple the Saviour came.
3. In the beautiful temple that's built on high,
Hosan - na! hosan - na!
Hosanna in the highest, ho-san - na!
And the balmy spring air with their voices rang.
And he smiled on the children who sang his name.
In the glo- rious cit - y beyond the sky,
Hosan - na! hosan - na!
Hosanna in the highest, ho-san - na!
A - gain spring is here with its sun - ny days, A - gain let the
A - gain he will come to his courts . . . be - low, A - gain he will
A - gain he will hear the rejoic - - ing song Of chil- dren who
Again spring is here with its sunny days, Again spring is here with its sunny days, Again let the children their
Again he will come to his courts below, Again he will come to his courts below, Again he will welcome the
Again he will hear the rejoicing soug, Again he will hear the rejoicing song Of children who love him, a
chil - dren their voi - ces raise In joy - ful cho - rus, in
wel - come the cheer - ful flow Of hymns as - cend - ing from
love him, a ran - somed throng, To him all wor - ship, all
voices raise, Again let the children their voices raise, In joyful chorus, in joyful chorus, In
cheerful flow, Again he will welcome the cheerful flow Of hymns ascending, of hymns ascending From
ransom'd throng, Of children who love him, a ransom'd throng, To him all worship, to him all worship, All

Hosanna in the Highest.—CONCLUDED.

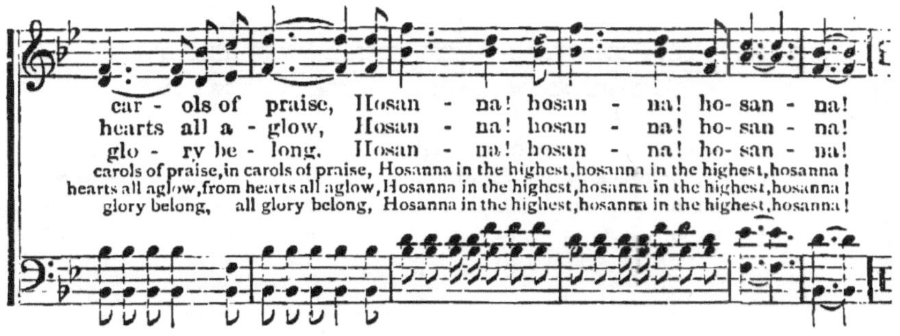
car - ols of praise, Hosan - na! hosan - na! ho- san - na!
hearts all a - glow, Hosan - na! hosan - na! ho- san - na!
glo - ry be - long, Hosan - na! hosan - na! ho- san - na!
carols of praise, in carols of praise, Hosanna in the highest, hosanna in the highest, hosanna!
hearts all aglow, from hearts all aglow, Hosanna in the highest, hosanna in the highest, hosanna!
glory belong, all glory belong, Hosanna in the highest, hosanna in the highest, hosanna!

America.

S. F. Smith.

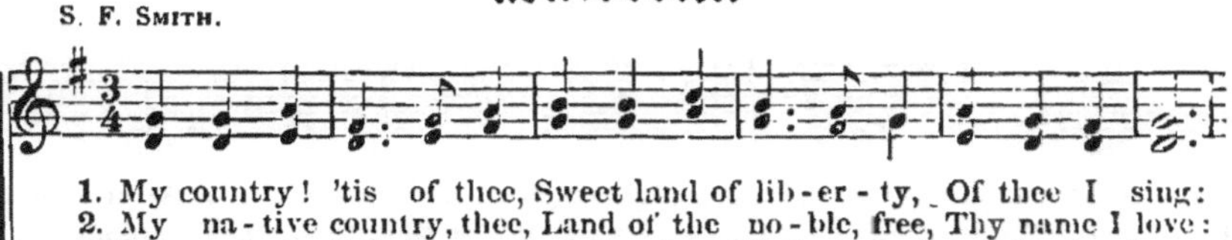

1. My country! 'tis of thee, Sweet land of lib - er - ty, Of thee I sing:
2. My na - tive country, thee, Land of the no - ble, free, Thy name I love:
3. Let music swell the breeze, And ring from all the trees Sweet freedom's song:

Land where my father's died! Land of the pilgrims' pride! From ev - 'ry
I love thy rocks and rills, Thy woods and templed hills: My heart with
Let mortal tongues a - wake; Let all that breathe partake; Let rocks their

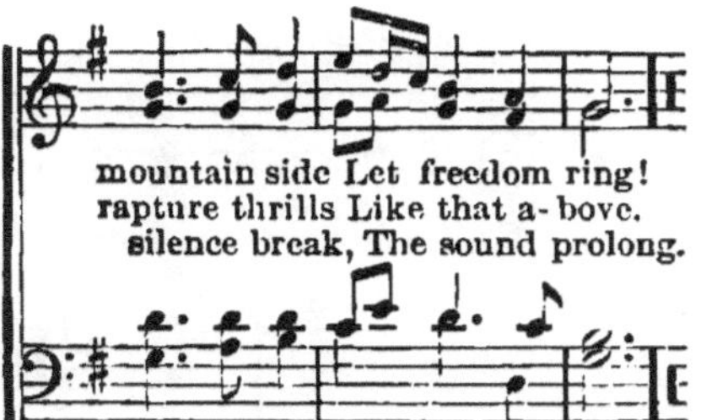
mountain side Let freedom ring!
rapture thrills Like that a - bove.
silence break, The sound prolong.

4 Our fathers' God! to thee,
Author of liberty,
To thee we sing:
Long may our land be bright
With freedom's holy light;
Protect us by thy might,
Great God, our King!

Remember the Sabbath Day.

E. A. Barnes. Ex. xx. 8. Wm. J. Kirkpatrick.

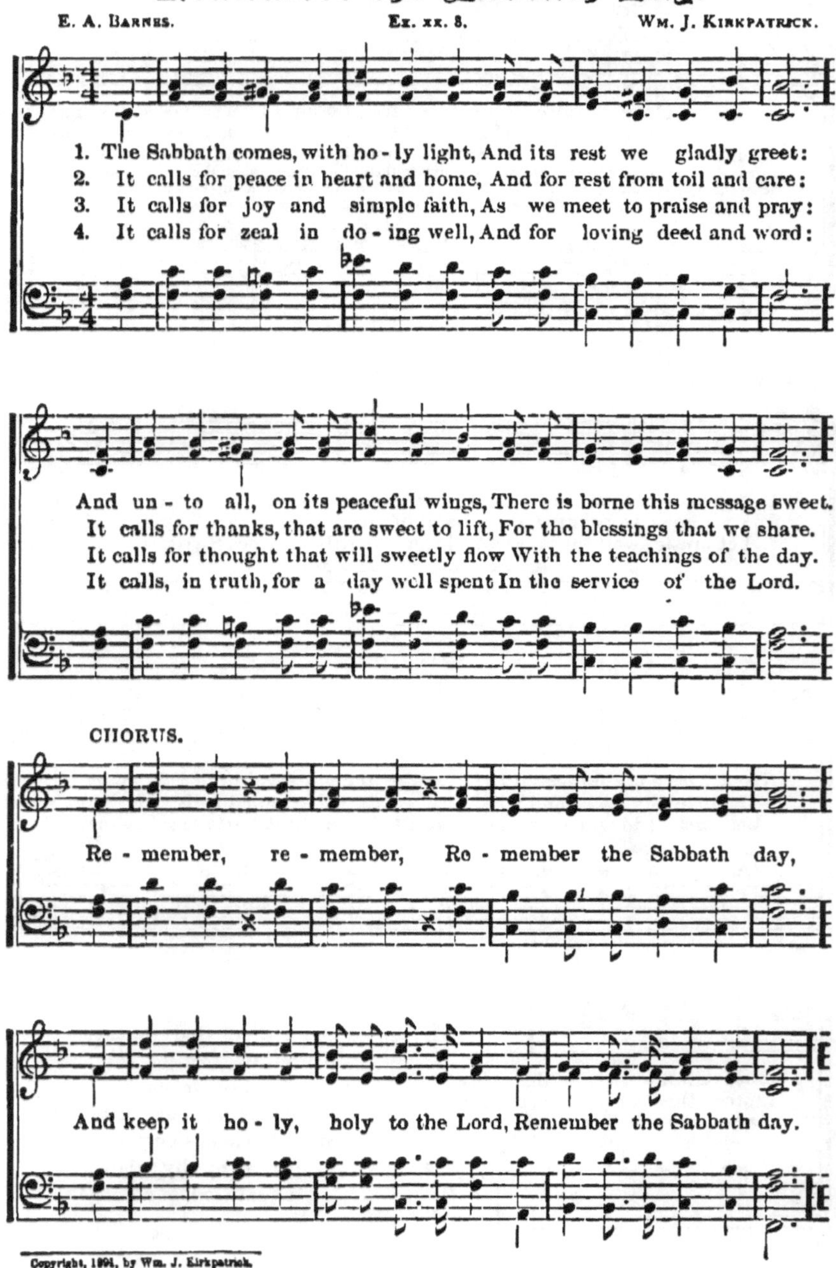
1. The Sabbath comes, with ho - ly light, And its rest we gladly greet:
2. It calls for peace in heart and home, And for rest from toil and care:
3. It calls for joy and simple faith, As we meet to praise and pray:
4. It calls for zeal in do - ing well, And for loving deed and word:
And un - to all, on its peaceful wings, There is borne this message sweet.
It calls for thanks, that are sweet to lift, For the blessings that we share.
It calls for thought that will sweetly flow With the teachings of the day.
It calls, in truth, for a day well spent In the service of the Lord.
CHORUS.
Re - member, re - member, Re - member the Sabbath day,
And keep it ho - ly, holy to the Lord, Remember the Sabbath day.

Trust and Obey.

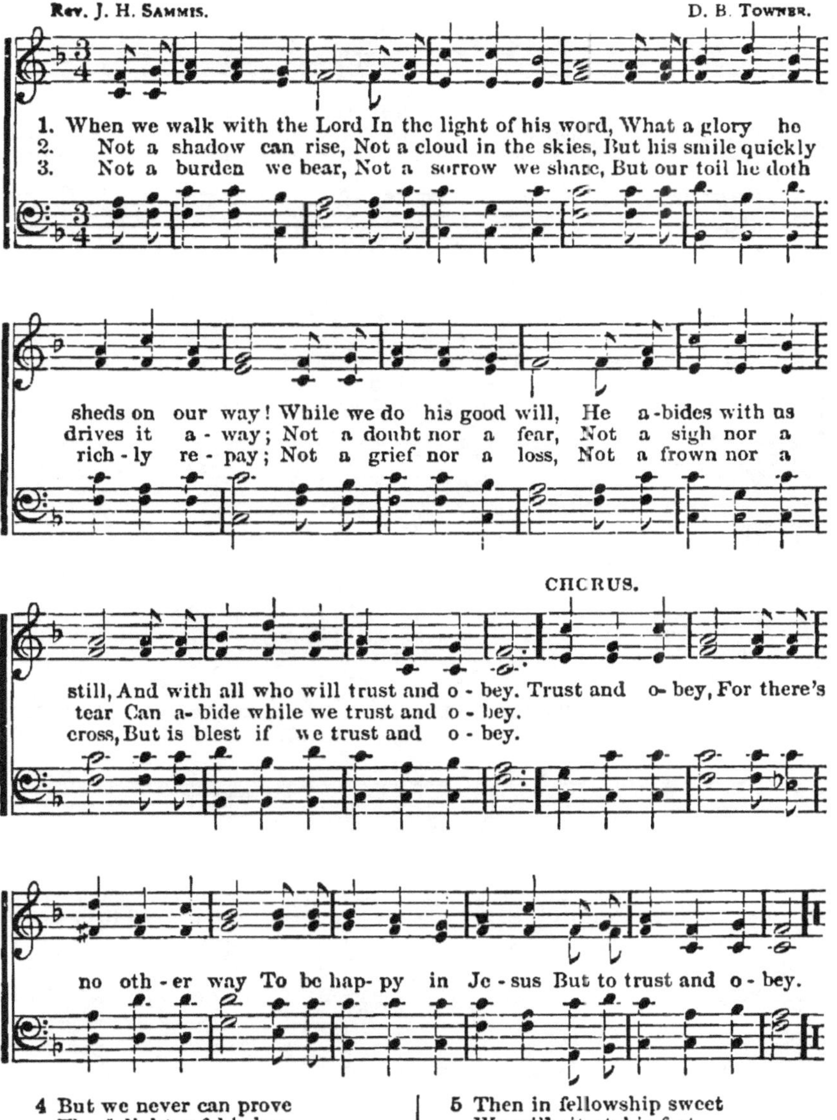
Rev. J. H. Sammis.
D. B. Towner.
1. When we walk with the Lord In the light of his word, What a glory he
2. Not a shadow can rise, Not a cloud in the skies, But his smile quickly
3. Not a burden we bear, Not a sorrow we share, But our toil he doth
sheds on our way! While we do his good will, He a-bides with us
drives it a-way; Not a doubt nor a fear, Not a sigh nor a
rich-ly re-pay; Not a grief nor a loss, Not a frown nor a
still, And with all who will trust and o-bey.
tear Can a-bide while we trust and o-bey.
cross, But is blest if we trust and o-bey.
CHORUS.
Trust and o-bey, For there's no oth-er way To be hap-py in Je-sus But to trust and o-bey.

4 But we never can prove
The delights of his love
Until all on the altar we lay,
For the favor he shows,
And the joy he bestows,
Are for all who will trust and obey.

5 Then in fellowship sweet
We will sit at his feet,
Or we'll walk by his side in the way;
What he says we will do,
Where he sends we will go,
Never fear, only trust and obey.

The Dear Heathen Girl.

Mrs. L. V. Haulman. Katie Flinder.

1. How can I be hap- py, How can I be gay, While o - ver the
2. No welcome awaits her, no deep tenderness Makes blessed the
3. "Ye shall suffer the lit- tle ones," Jesus hath said, "To come un - to
wide, rolling sea, From the myri - ad islands and lands far remote
day of her birth, No place has the maiden, no joy and no love,
me and be blessed," But how can they come who know naught of the way
Sweet voi - ces are calling to me; From a-far where the ice-peaks
No honor in heaven or on earth; Oh, my heart, how it thrills with its
To the Saviour who lov- ing - ly pressed To the heart of a God all the
rear their heads, Or the Gan - ges laps and purls, With sobs and with
pit- y and pain! How I long those strong shackles to hurl To the darkness that
little ones? then, Oh, send where the forest smoke curls, Send hope to the
pleadings for life and for hope Comes the voice of the dear heathen girl.
forged them, and out of the gloom Of her night lead the dear heathen girl.
mountains and deserts and plains, Send Christ to the dear heathen girl.

Go ye into All the World.
F. G. Burroughs.
Adam Geibel.
1. "Go ye into all the world!" Hear the Lord's command; Bear the light of gos - pel truth To each darkened land; Draw the shades of un - be- lief From their blinded eyes,—Let the Sun of Righteousness With healing rise!
2. "Go ye in - to all the world!" Heed his last command; Do not let the nations die While ye waiting stand; From your Saviour's pierced hands Take the bread of life, Car - ry ye the food abroad Where need is rife.
3. "Go ye in - to all the world!" Gladly we o - bey, Sending forth the bless - ed news, "Christ is risen to - day!" From the darkness of the past God has rolled the stone: Lo! upon the distant isles His sun has shone.
Chorus.
He shall reign, he shall reign, Who hath triumphed o'er the grave; He shall reign, he shall reign, Christ the Victor, strong to save!
He shall reign, he shall reign,
He shall reign, he shall reign,
strong to save!

The Blessing of Song.

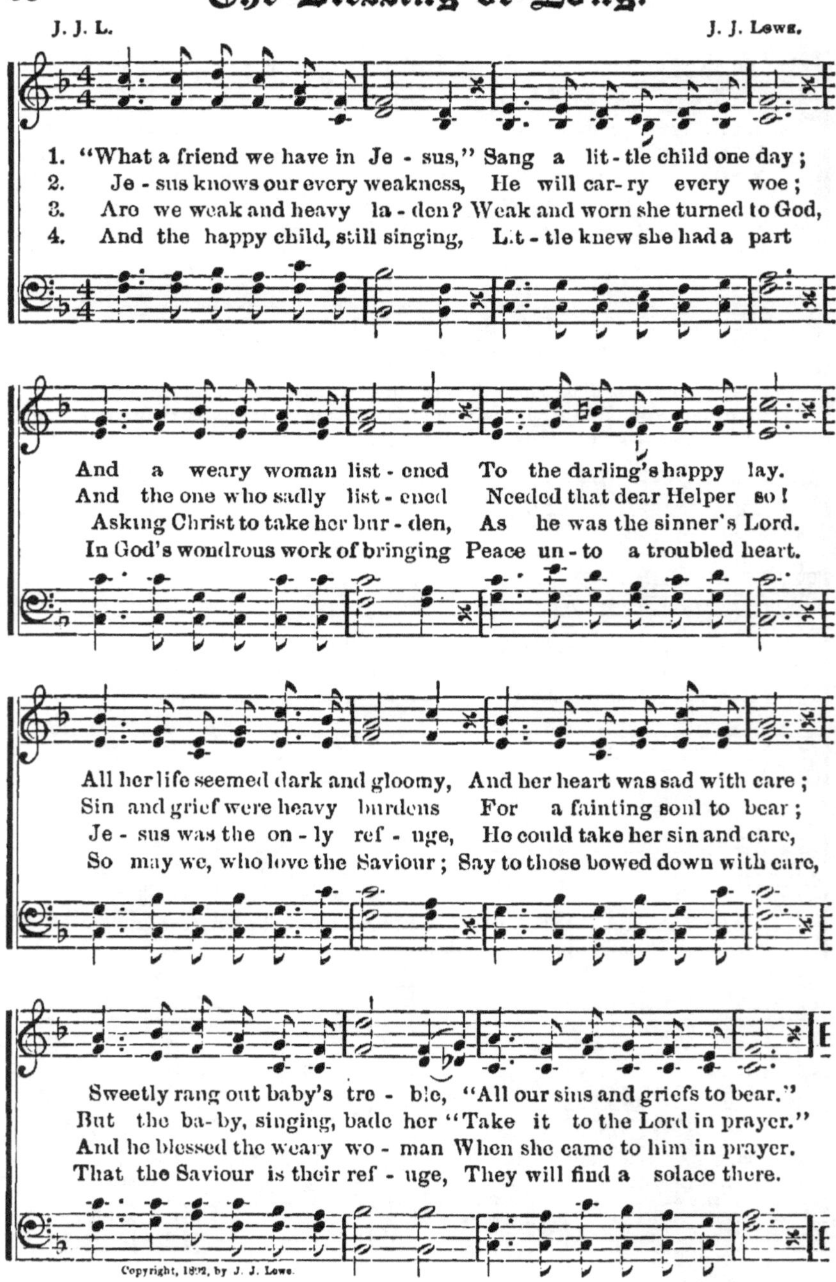
J. J. L.
J. J. Lowe.
1. "What a friend we have in Je - sus," Sang a lit - tle child one day;
2. Je - sus knows our every weakness, He will car - ry every woe;
3. Are we weak and heavy la - den? Weak and worn she turned to God,
4. And the happy child, still singing, Lit - tle knew she had a part
And a weary woman list - ened To the darling's happy lay.
And the one who sadly list - ened Needed that dear Helper so!
Asking Christ to take her bur - den, As he was the sinner's Lord.
In God's wondrous work of bringing Peace un - to a troubled heart.
All her life seemed dark and gloomy, And her heart was sad with care;
Sin and grief were heavy burdens For a fainting soul to bear;
Je - sus was the on - ly ref - uge, He could take her sin and care,
So may we, who love the Saviour; Say to those bowed down with care,
Sweetly rang out baby's tre - ble, "All our sins and griefs to bear."
But the ba - by, singing, bade her "Take it to the Lord in prayer."
And he blessed the weary wo - man When she came to him in prayer.
That the Saviour is their ref - uge, They will find a solace there.

Anywhere With Jesus.

Jessie H. Brown. "I will trust and not be afraid." Isaiah xii. 2. D. B. Towner. By per.

1. An- ywhere with Je- sus I can safe - ly go, An- ywhere He
2. An- ywhere with Je- sus I am not a - lone, Other friends may
3. An- ywhere with Je- sus I can go to sleep, When the darkling

leads me in this world be - low. Anywhere without him, dearest
fail me, He is still my own. Tho' his hand may lead me o - ver
shadows round a- bout me creep; Knowing I shall waken nev - er

joys would fade, Anywhere with Je- sus I am not a - fraid.
drearest ways, Anywhere with Je- sus is a house of praise.
more to roam, Anywhere with Je- sus will be home, sweet home.

CHORUS.

An - y - where! an - y - where! Fear I can - not know,
An - y - where with Je - sus I can safe - ly go.

Plant Roses.

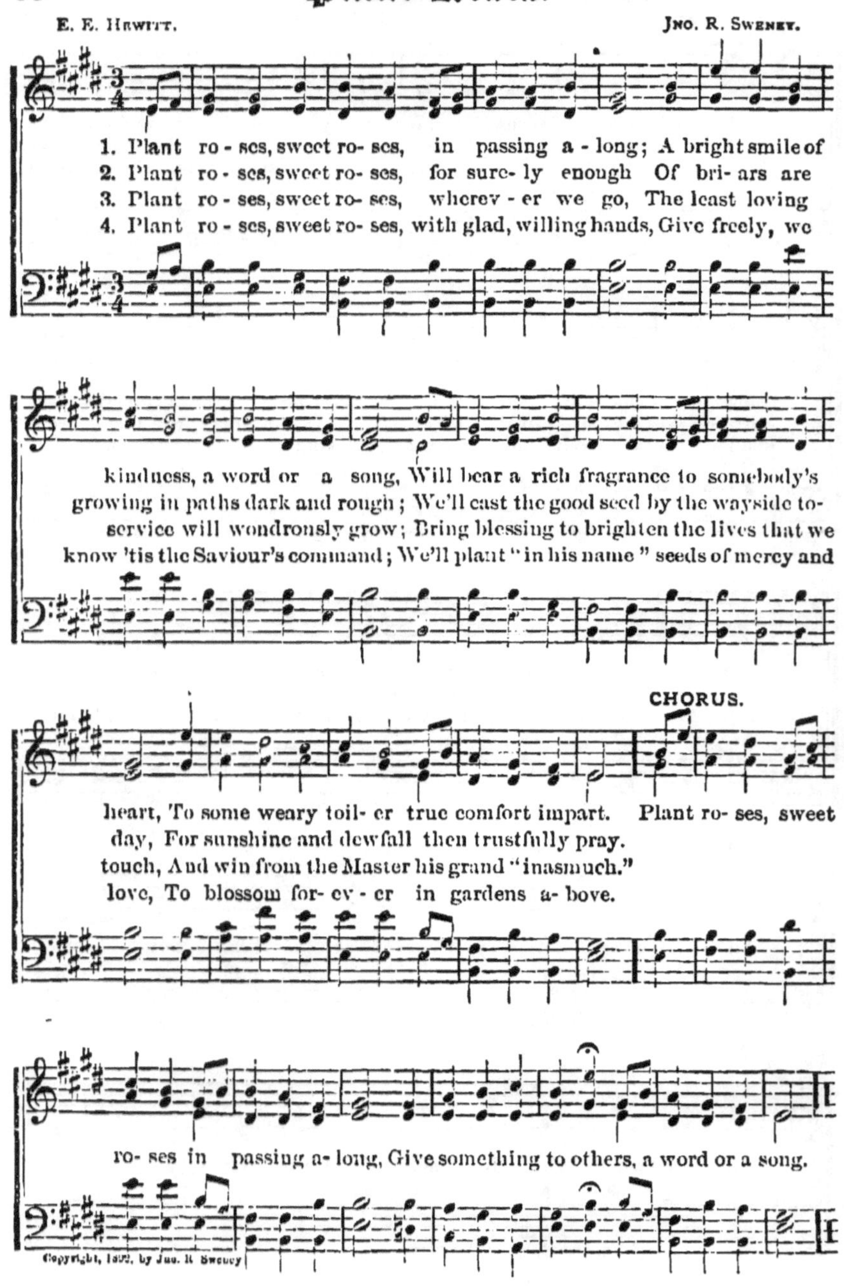
E. E. Hewitt.
Jno. R. Sweney.
1. Plant ro - ses, sweet ro- ses, in passing a - long; A bright smile of
2. Plant ro - ses, sweet ro- ses, for sure- ly enough Of bri- ars are
3. Plant ro - ses, sweet ro- ses, wherev - er we go, The least loving
4. Plant ro - ses, sweet ro- ses, with glad, willing hands, Give freely, we
kindness, a word or a song, Will bear a rich fragrance to somebody's
growing in paths dark and rough; We'll cast the good seed by the wayside to-
service will wondrously grow; Bring blessing to brighten the lives that we
know 'tis the Saviour's command; We'll plant "in his name" seeds of mercy and
heart, To some weary toil- er true comfort impart.
day, For sunshine and dewfall then trustfully pray.
touch, And win from the Master his grand "inasmuch."
love, To blossom for- ev - er in gardens a- bove.
CHORUS.
Plant ro- ses, sweet ro- ses in passing a- long, Give something to others, a word or a song.
Copyright, 1892, by Jno. R. Sweney

Entire Consecration.

FRANCES RIDLEY HAVERGAL. Chorus by W. J. K. WM. J. KIRKPATRICK.

1. Take my life, and let it be Con - se - crat - ed, Lord, to thee;
2. Take my feet, and let them be Swift and beau - ti - ful for thee;
3. Take my lips, and let them be Filled with mes - sag - es for thee;
4. Take my moments and my days, Let them flow in endless praise;
Take my hands and let them move At the impulse of thy love.
Take my voice and let me sing Al - ways, on - ly, for my King.
Take my sil - ver and my gold,— Not a mite would I withhold.
Take my in - tel - lect, and use Ev - 'ry power as thou shalt choose.
CHORUS.
Wash me in the Saviour's precious blood, the precious blood,
Cleanse me in its pu - ri - fy - ing flood, the healing flood,
Lord, I give to
thee, my life and all, to be, Thine, henceforth, e - ter - nal - ly.

5 Take my will, and make it thine;
It shall be no longer mine;
Take my heart,—it is thine own,—
It shall be thy royal throne.

6 Take my love,—my Lord, I pour
At thy feet its treasure-store!
Take myself, and I will be
Ever, only, all for thee!

Upward, Growing Upward.

E. E. Hewitt. Adam Geibel.

1. "Upward, growing upward," say the blooming flow'rs, Rousing from the slumber
2. We are growing upward, happy children say, More and more like Jesus,
of the snowy hours; Aid- ed by the dew-drops rain, and sunshine fair,
growing ev- 'ry day; Ev - er marching onward in the paths of light,
Kindly cheered and welcomed by the balmy air. "Upward," sings the birdie,
Trusting, sweetly trusting in the Saviour's might. Jesus gives us sunshine,
in his joyous flight, Soaring, soaring gayly upward in the morning bright;
teaching like the dew, Loves to see his children growing faithful, kind, and true;
"Farewell, lit - tle blossoms, I must seek the blue, Then I'll send a
Day by day we're marching to the home a - bove, Growing in the

CHORUS.
merry car - ol down to you. Upward! upward! children, too, are
beauty of the Lord we love.
singing Upward! upward! hap- py voi- ces ringing; Upward! upward!
glad hosannas bringing; Like the birds and blossoms we will seek the light.
Earnest Prayer.
Rev. Chas. Roads.
Wm. J. Kirkpatrick.
1. Je - sus comes with sav-ing grace To a child in ear - nest prayer,
2. Je - sus ev - er stands be-side Ev - 'ry child in ear - nest prayer!
3. Je - sus light and pow'r will give To a child in ear - nest prayer!
And re - veals his lov - ing face,—Helps him ev - 'ry - where!
Sends the Spir - it to a - bide,— And for work pre - pare!
In his righteous - ness to live, And his glo - ry share!

Steady, Steady, Loyal Soldiers.

E. E. Hewitt. Wm. J. Kirkpatrick.

1. Nev - er will the Master leave us, Nev - er will his promise fail;
On - ly let us press the clos - er When the pow'rs of sin as - sail.

2. In our mighty Christian ar - my There's a part for us to do;
Hold a - loft the gos - pel ban - ner, Cheerful - ly the pledge re - new.

3. When we wholly trust in Je - sus, When our hearts in love outflow,
We will learn the happy se - cret Of a blessed life be - low.

4. Let us render willing ser - vice, Glad - ly answer, "here am I;"
We are marching on to glo - ry, Singing of our home on high.

CHORUS.

Steady, steady, loy - al soldiers, Take your or - ders day by day;
True and faithful, fol - low Je - sus, Fol - low all the way.

Sing Praises, Happy Praises.

Delia T. White.
Jno. R. Sweney.
BOYS.
1. Sing praises, happy praises, Come, sing and rejoice; To God, our heav'nly
2. Sing praises, happy praises, Come, sing and rejoice; To Je - sus, blessed
3. Sing praises, happy praises, Come, sing and rejoice; To God, the Ho - ly
GIRLS.
Father, Lift up heart and voice. He made us, defends us With wisdom and might;
Saviour, Lift up heart and voice. He lov'd us and sought us, He left his bright throne;
Spirit, Lift up heart and voice. He comforts us sweetly, The kind, gentle Dove;
CHORUS.
Rich blessing he sends us By day and by night. His mercy fails us nev - er,
With precious blood bought us, And made us his own.
He'll fit us complete- ly For glo- ry above.
While at the cross we bend; Sing praises, happy praises, To our best friend.
Copyright, 1882, by Jno. R. Sweney.

By the Seaside.

W. L. M. W. L. Mason.

1. See the bless - ed Saviour teaching, By the sea of Gal - i - lee,
2. Hear the sto - ry of the sow-er,—Seed he casts by way-side high,
3. So the les - son comes with power, Comes to all with ears to hear,
Les - sons that are still far-reaching. For they help to make men free,—
Some on ground a lit - tle low- er, Fall a - mong the rocks to die.
Seed are be - ing sown each hour, Bearing fruit- age year by year.
Free from sin and free from sorrow, For as through this world we go,
Oth - er seed the bram- ble smothers, But that sown on fer - tile soil,
Hearts are ev - ery-where re- ceiv- ing, Seeds of right and seeds of wrong;
None can tell what on the morrow, May be his of weal or woe.
Un - like an - y of the oth- ers, Well re- pays the farmer's toil.
But in Je - sus Christ believ - ing, We shall join the angel's song.
CHORUS.
All are sow- ing, some are reaping, Soon the sheaves shall gathered be;

Are you in your mem- 'ry keeping, Je - sus' words in Gal - i - lee?

The Wondrous Story.

J. E. FARNSWORTH. W. L. MASON.

1. Oh, hear the wondrous story : Sing, children, sing! Came Christ the Lord of
2. One day when many sought him,—Sing, children, sing! Mothers their children
3. Then in his arms he clasped them,—Sing, children, sing! And with his smile he
4. Come, give your hearts to Jesus,—Sing, children, sing! His gracious eye still

glo - ry,—Sing, children, sing! Came here to bring us blessing, For
brought him,—Sing, children, sing! Though some had rudely chid them, He
blessed them,—Sing, children, sing! "Of such" said he, "is heav- en; All
sees us,—Sing, children, sing! Nought from his love can sev - er, And

us his love confess - ing, Love which is never ceasing; Sing, children, sing!
said "Do not forbid them," And in his breast he hid them; Sing, children, sing!
must be little children, To such my wisdom's given,"—Sing, children, sing!
when this life is o - ver, We will his praise forever Sing, children, sing!

Let Us Endeavor.

E. E. Hewitt. Wm. J. Kirkpatrick.

1. Let us endeav - or to speak for the Master; Surely he's worthy our heart-i - est praise; Worthy our loyal and loving con-fes -sion; Worthy the hymns of thanksgiving we raise.
2. Let us endeav - or to work for the Master; Serving in gladness wher- ev - er we go, Keeping our lamps shining out in the darkness, Till others fol - low the heaven- lit glow.
3. Let us endeav - or to live for the Master; Live for his glo - ry who died for our sin; Yielding our all in a true con- se- cra- tion, Trusting, o - bey - ing, his blessing we win.
CHORUS.
Help - ing us ev - er In each endeav - or, Je - sus stands by us to give us suc- cess; His arm upholding, His love en -
Helping us ev - er, In each endeavor,
Helping us ev - er, In each endeavor, Jesus stands by us to give us success,
Jesus stands by us to give us success;

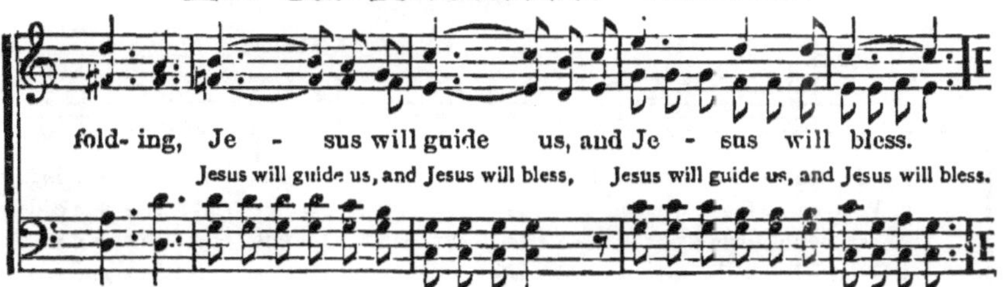
fold- ing, Je - sus will guide us, and Je - sus will bless.
Jesus will guide us, and Jesus will bless, Jesus will guide us, and Jesus will bless.

Little Ones Like Me.

JNO. R. SWENEY.

1. Je- sus, when he left the sky, And for sinners came to die, In his mer- cy passed not by Little ones like me.
2. Mothers then the Saviour sought In the places where he taught, And to him the children brought, Little ones like me.
3. Did the Saviour say them nay? No, he kindly bade them stay, Suffered none to turn a - way Little ones like me.
4. 'Twas for them his life he gave, To redeem them from the grave, Jesus now will gladly save Little ones like me.

CHORUS.

Little ones, little ones, "Suffer them to come," said he; Jesus loves the little ones, Little ones like me.

Jesus the Children's Friend.

W. L. M.
W. L. Mason.
SOLO.
CHORUS.
1. I won - der who is the children's friend? Je- sus is! Je - sus is!
2. Who came from heaven for us to die? Je- sus did! Je - sus did!
3. O who was cru - ci - fied for sin? Je- sus was! Je - sus was!
4. And who will love us while life shall last? Je- sus will! Je - sus will!
SOLO.
CHORUS.
Who will love them to the end? Je - sus, on - ly Je - sus.
Who was lift - ed up on high? Je - sus, on - ly Je - sus.
Who for us did heav - en win? Je - sus, on - ly Je - sus.
Who will take us home at last? Je - sus, on - ly Je - sus.
CHORUS.
Tell, oh, tell of Je - sus' praise! Loud and clear your voi - ces raise!
Up to him our songs as - cend, Je - sus is our friend.

Loving Each Other.

D. E. L. "Let us love one another."—1 John iv : 1. D. E. Lorenz. By per.

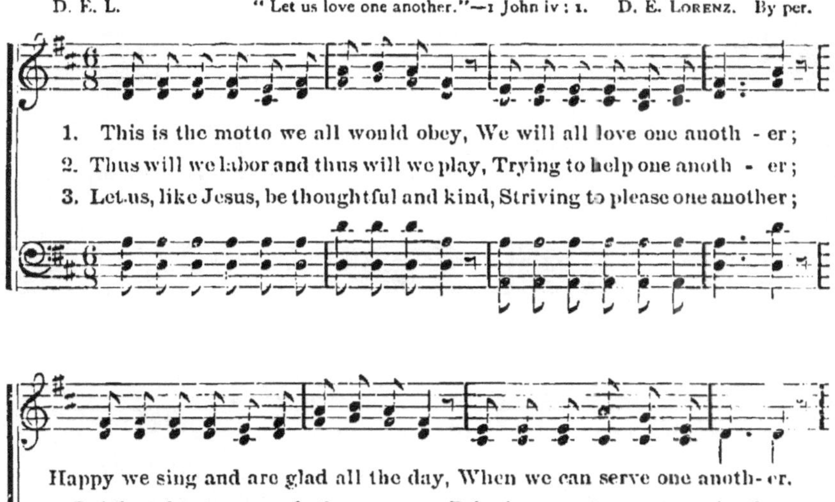
1. This is the motto we all would obey, We will all love one anoth - er;
2. Thus will we labor and thus will we play, Trying to help one anoth - er;
3. Let us, like Jesus, be thoughtful and kind, Striving to please one another;
Happy we sing and are glad all the day, When we can serve one anoth- er.
Driving the sorrows of others away, Bringing sweet peace to each other.
Here, as in heav'n, we will be of one mind, Ev'ry one loving the oth - er.

CHORUS.

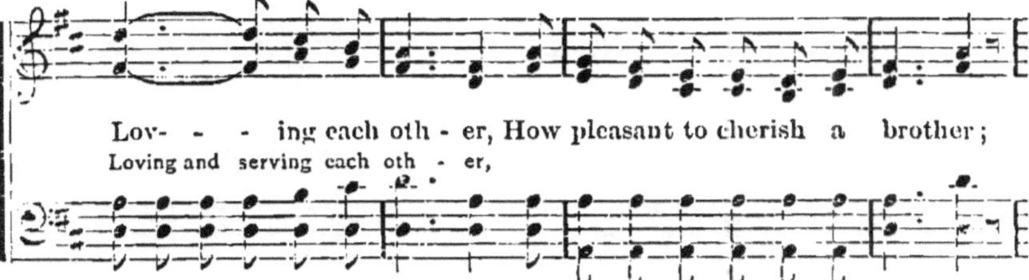
Lov- - - ing each oth - er, How pleasant to cherish a brother;
Loving and serving each oth - er,

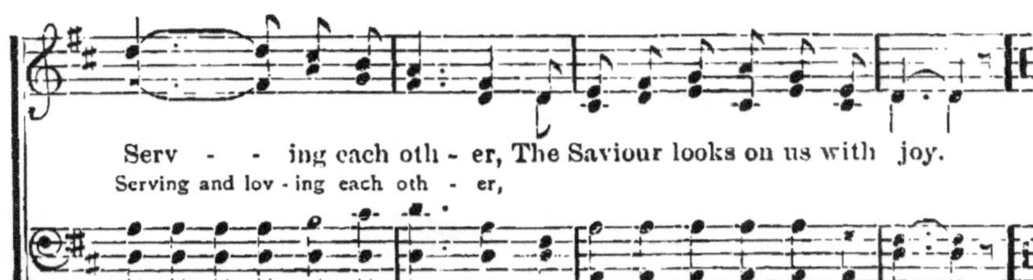
Serv - - ing each oth - er, The Saviour looks on us with joy.
Serving and lov - ing each oth - er,

More about Jesus.

E. E. Hewitt. Jno. R. Sweney.

1. More about Je-sus would I know, More of his grace to oth-ers show:
2. More about Je-sus let me learn, More of his ho - ly will discern;
3. More about Je-sus; in his word, Holding communion with my Lord;
4. More about Je-sus; on his throne, Riches in glo - ry all his own;

More of his sav-ing ful-ness see, More of his love who died for me.
Spir - it of God, my teacher be, Showing the things of Christ to me.
Hearing his voice in ev - 'ry line, Making each faithful say-ing mine.
More of his kingdom's sure increase; More of his coming, Prince of Peace.

REFRAIN.

More, more a-bout Je - sus, More, more a-bout Je - sus;
More of his sav-ing ful-ness see, More of his love who died for me.

Jesus for Me.

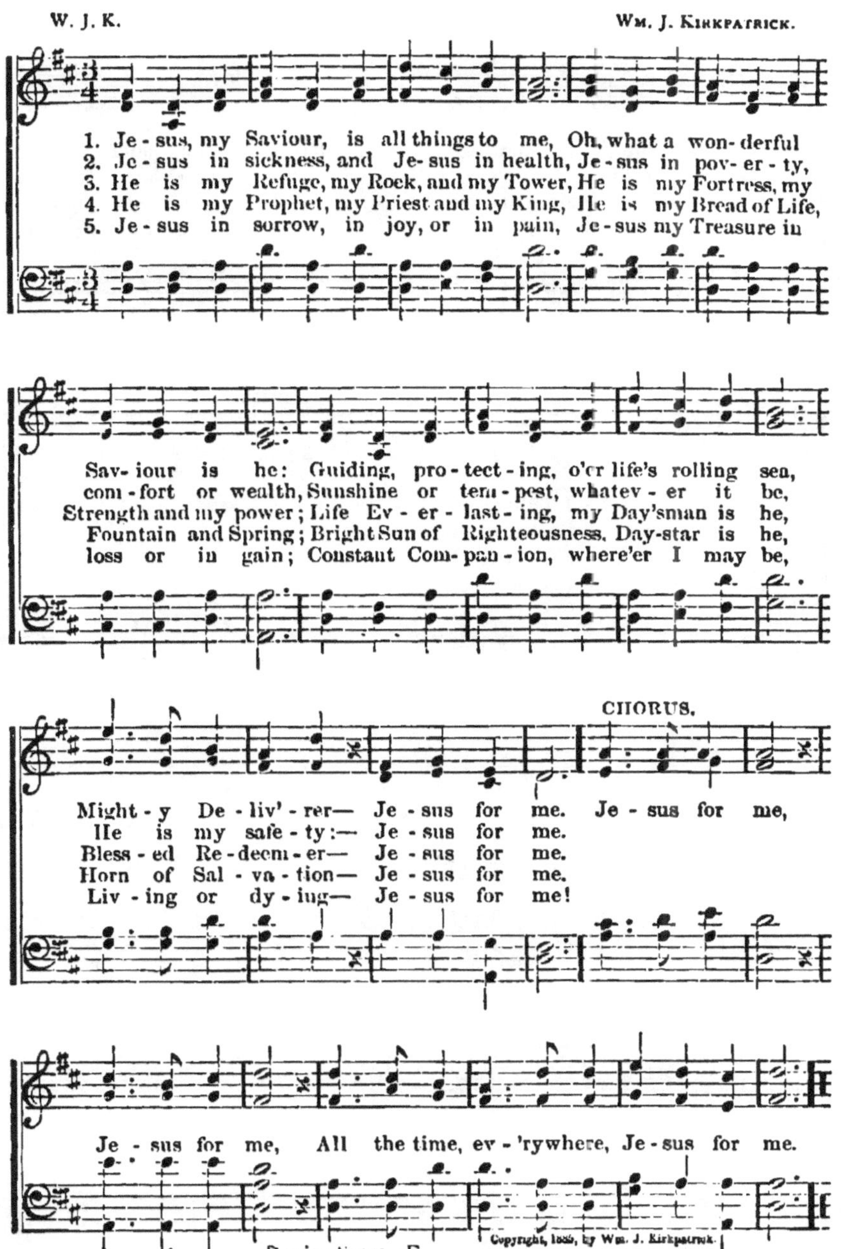
W. J. K.
Wm. J. Kirkpatrick.
1. Je - sus, my Saviour, is all things to me, Oh, what a won- derful
2. Je - sus in sickness, and Je - sus in health, Je - sus in pov - er - ty,
3. He is my Refuge, my Rock, and my Tower, He is my Fortress, my
4. He is my Prophet, my Priest and my King, He is my Bread of Life,
5. Je - sus in sorrow, in joy, or in pain, Je - sus my Treasure in
Sav- iour is he: Guiding, pro - tect - ing, o'er life's rolling sea,
com - fort or wealth, Sunshine or tem - pest, whatev - er it be,
Strength and my power; Life Ev - er - last - ing, my Day'sman is he,
Fountain and Spring; Bright Sun of Righteousness, Day-star is he,
loss or in gain; Constant Com- pan - ion, where'er I may be,
Might - y De - liv' - rer— Je - sus for me.
He is my safe - ty:— Je - sus for me.
Bless - ed Re - deem - er— Je - sus for me.
Horn of Sal - va - tion— Je - sus for me.
Liv - ing or dy - ing— Je - sus for me!
CHORUS.
Je - sus for me,
Je - sus for me, All the time, ev - 'rywhere, Je - sus for me.
Copyright, 1886, by Wm. J. Kirkpatrick.

The Mission Band.

E. E. Hewitt.
Jno. R. Sweney.
1. Come and join our mission band, Come and lend a helping hand, Sending
2. Man - y children far a - way, Nev - er to "our Father" pray, No sweet
3. These poor children do not know, When they see the blossoms grow, That "our
4. Let us give, and work, and pray, For the children far a - way, And the
CHORUS.
out to ev- 'ry land, Tidings of our King. We will send abroad the gospel
Bi- ble verses say, No glad praises sing.
Father" made them so, Made the birds to sing.
last command obey Of our Saviour King.
sto - ry, Glad - ly send the precious gos- pel sto - ry, Tell the world of
Jesus and his glo - ry, We will tell the wondrous love of Christ our King.
Copyright, 1892, by Jno. R. Sweney.

Jesus has Died to Redeem Thee.

J. E. H. J. E. Hall.

1. Wonderful message that's sent unto me, Je- sus has died to redeem thee;
2. Hear what the message is saying to-day, Je- sus has died to redeem thee;
3. Hear it, O sinner, this message of love, Je- sus has died to redeem thee;
4. Give unto others the message you hear, Je- sus has died to redeem thee;
Message of love, and a message so free, Je- sus has died to redeem thee.
All who believe, oh, how blessed are they, Je- sus has died to redeem thee.
Sent down to earth from the heavens above, Je- sus has died to redeem thee.
Fill the sad earth with the words of good cheer, Je- sus has died to redeem thee.
CHORUS.
Je- sus has died to redeem thee, Send the glad message the needy world o'er;
he has died to redeem,
Je- sus has died to redeem thee, Proclaim it the needy world o'er.
he has died to redeem,

Blessed be the Name.

W. H. CLARK. Arranged by WM. J. KIRKPATRICK.

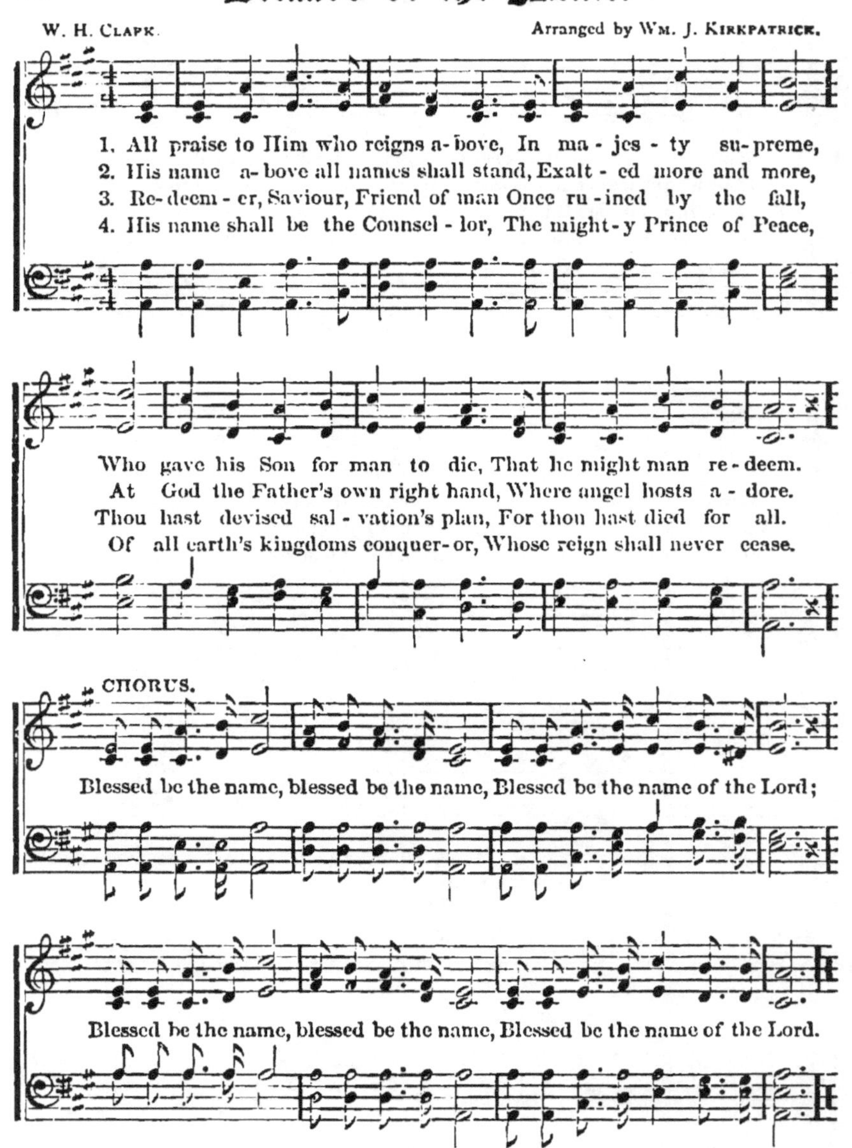
1. All praise to Him who reigns a-bove, In ma-jes-ty su-preme,
2. His name a-bove all names shall stand, Exalt-ed more and more,
3. Re-deem-er, Saviour, Friend of man Once ru-ined by the fall,
4. His name shall be the Counsel-lor, The might-y Prince of Peace,
Who gave his Son for man to die, That he might man re-deem.
At God the Father's own right hand, Where angel hosts a-dore.
Thou hast devised sal-vation's plan, For thou hast died for all.
Of all earth's kingdoms conquer-or, Whose reign shall never cease.
CHORUS.
Blessed be the name, blessed be the name, Blessed be the name of the Lord;
Blessed be the name, blessed be the name, Blessed be the name of the Lord.

5 The ransomed hosts to thee shall bring
Their praise and homage meet;
With rapturous awe adore their King,
And worship at his feet.

6 Then shall we know as we are known,
And in that world above
Forever sing around the throne
His everlasting love.

'Tis Sweet to Confess Him.

E. E. Hewitt. Jno. R. Sweney.

1. 'Tis sweet to confess him, our Master and Guide, To ring it out boldly, we're
2. 'Tis sweet to confess him, our Saviour and Friend, To speak of the mercies that
3. 'Tis sweet to confess him, that others may hear How good is our Jesus, how
4. 'Tis sweet to confess him, someday he will come With all his bright angels to
on the Lord's side; To lift up his banner, and gratefully show, Where
nev - er shall end; To pass on the message that cheered us to-day, Our
gracious and dear; To tell his sal - va- tion, our ransom from sin, The
gath- er us home, And those who have faithful- ly witnessed be- low, Shall
D.S.—fling out his banner, and let the world know, Where
Je- sus shall lead us we're willing to go.
neighbor, perhaps, it will help on the way.
might of his Spir- it a - biding with- in.
rise in his likeness, his glo- ry shall know.
Fine.
CHORUS.
O joyful- ly praise him! O
Je- sus shall lead us we're willing to go.
trustful - ly sing, 'Tis sweet to confess him, our Saviour and King; We'll
D. S.

I. WATTS. "Look unto me, and be ye saved,"—Isa. xlv. 22. R. E. HUDSON.

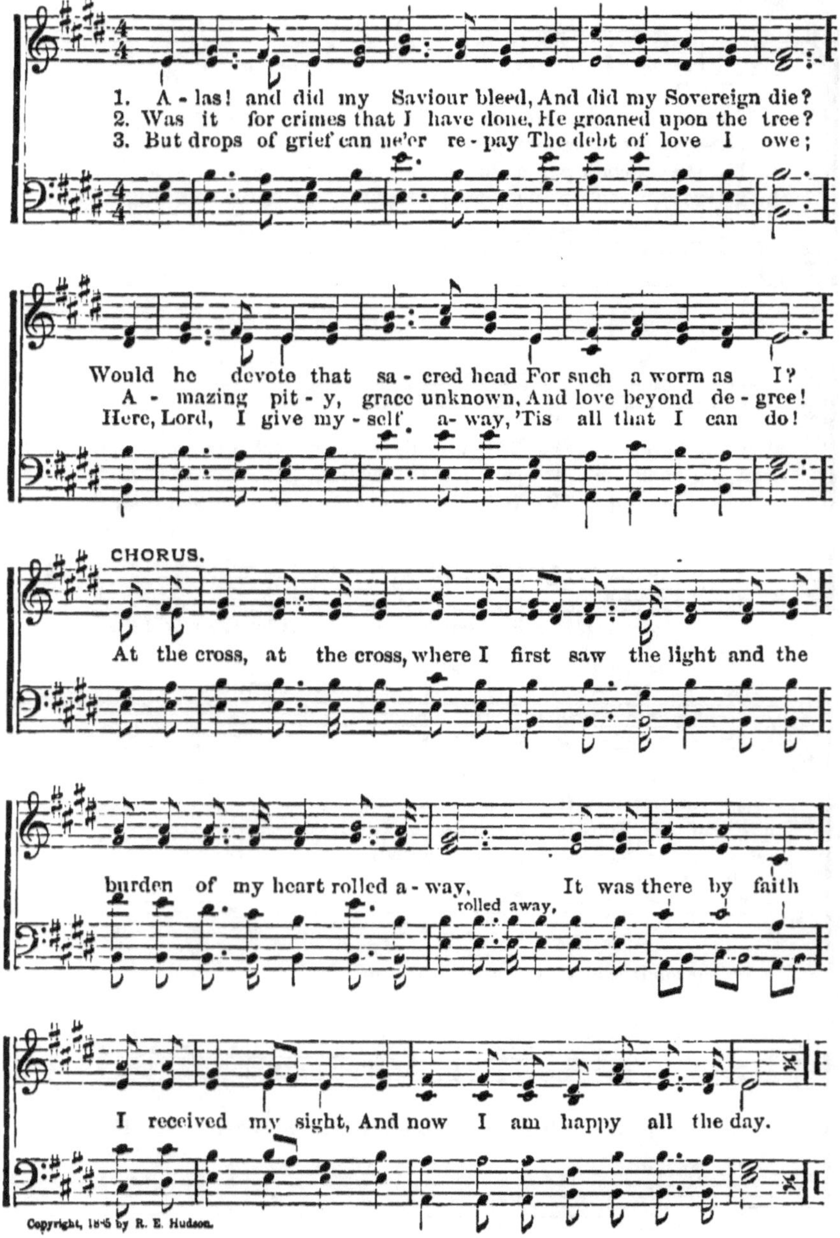

1. A - las! and did my Saviour bleed, And did my Sovereign die?
Would he devote that sa - cred head For such a worm as I?

2. Was it for crimes that I have done, He groaned upon the tree?
A - mazing pit - y, grace unknown, And love beyond de - gree!

3. But drops of grief can ne'er re - pay The debt of love I owe;
Here, Lord, I give my - self a - way, 'Tis all that I can do!

CHORUS.

At the cross, at the cross, where I first saw the light and the burden of my heart rolled a - way, (rolled away,) It was there by faith I received my sight, And now I am happy all the day.

The Very Same Jesus. 87

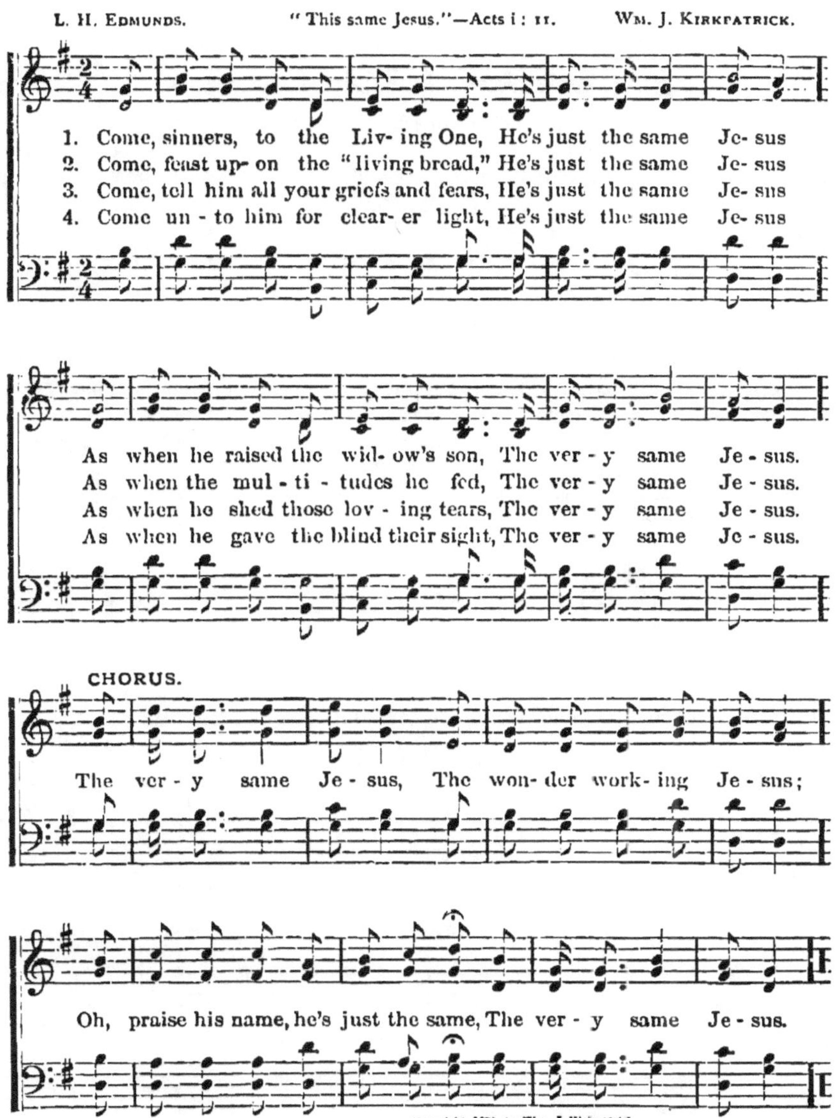
L. H. Edmunds.
"This same Jesus."—Acts i : 11.
Wm. J. Kirkpatrick.
1. Come, sinners, to the Liv- ing One, He's just the same Je- sus
2. Come, feast up- on the "living bread," He's just the same Je- sus
3. Come, tell him all your griefs and fears, He's just the same Je- sus
4. Come un - to him for clear- er light, He's just the same Je- sus
As when he raised the wid- ow's son, The ver - y same Je - sus.
As when the mul - ti - tudes he fed, The ver - y same Je - sus.
As when he shed those lov - ing tears, The ver - y same Je - sus.
As when he gave the blind their sight, The ver - y same Je - sus.
CHORUS.
The ver - y same Je - sus, The won- der work- ing Je - sus;
Oh, praise his name, he's just the same, The ver - y same Je - sus.

5 Calm 'midst the waves of trouble be,
He's just the same Jesus
As when he hushed the raging sea,
The very same Jesus.

6 Some day our raptured eyes shall see
He's just the same Jesus;
Oh, blessed day for you and me!
The very same Jesus.

We're a Happy Band.

ELIZABETH STILLWELL.
ADAM GEIBEL
1. We're a happy band of pilgrims, bound for glory, We are marching in the bright and shining way; Come, oh, come and sing with us salvation's sto - ry, Come, and seek the land of ev - er - lasting day.
2. Tho' the mighty powers of sin shall oft as- sail us, Tho' the subtle snare be spread around our feet, Let us look to Jesus, he will never fail us, We are trusting in his promise, sure and sweet.
3. Tho' we walk at times beneath the clouds of sorrow, Still the bow of blessing spans the heaven's o'er, At the dawning of the glad and golden morrow, We shall stand beyond the shadows ev- ermore.
CHORUS.
We're a happy band of pilgrims, halle - lujah! We will sing redeeming mercy, o'er and o'er; We are marching on to glory, hallelujah, In the blessed path that shineth more and more.
Copyright, 1892, by John J. Hood.

Happy in the Love of Jesus.

Henrietta E. Blair. Wm. J. Kirkpatrick.

1. Bright is the day-star shin-ing for me, Happy in the love of Je - sus;
Now from my bondage grace makes me free, Happy in the love of Je - sus.

2. He has redeemed me, I am his own, Happy in the love of Je - sus;
Drawn by his mer-cy near to his throne, Happy in the love of Je - sus.

3. How I am honored, how I am blest, Happy in the love of Je - sus;
Un - der his ban - ner sweet-ly I rest, Happy in the love of Je - sus.

4. Firm is my anchor, steadfast and sure, Happy in the love of Je - sus;
All things with patience I can endure, Happy in the love of Je - sus.

CHORUS.

Praise from my full heart loudly shall ring, Born of the Spirit, child of a King;
Heir to his glo - ry, now will I sing,—Happy in the love of Je - sus.

Who will Follow Jesus?

E. E. Hewitt. Wm. J. Kirkpatrick.

1. Who will follow Je - sus, Standing for the right, Holding up his banner
2. Who will follow Je - sus In life's busy ways, Working for the Master,
3. Who will follow Jesus? When the tempter charms, Fleeing then, for safety
4. Who will follow Je - sus In his work of love? Leading others to him,
In the thickest fight? List'ning for his or - ders, Read- y to o- bey,
Giving him the praise? Earnest in his vineyard, Hon- or- ing his laws,
To the Saviour's arms; Trusting in his mer - cy, Trusting in his power,
Lifting prayers above; Courage, faithful servant; In his word we see,
Who will follow Je - sus, Serving him to-day?
Faithful to his counsel, Watchful for his cause?
Seeking fresh renewals Of his grace each hour.
On our side forev - er Will this Saviour be.
CHORUS.
Who will follow Je- sus?
Who will make reply, "I am on the Lord's side, Master, here am I?" Who will follow
Je- sus? Who will make reply, "I am on the Lord's side, Master, here am I?"

Be a Worker for the Lord.

E. A. Barnes.
Jno. R. Sweney.
1. Work, and let the Master see Read- y hand and willing heart; Work to bear his message sweet, And its rich - es to impart.
2. Work to storm the fort of sin, And to set the captives free; Work to speed the Master's cause O - ver land and o - ver sea.
3. Work to car - ry out his plan, That to all his truth may come; Work to bear the gospel hope To the waiting heart and home.
4. Work to sow the precious seed All a- long the passing years; Work to have your sheaves in hand When the harvest morn appears.
rit.
CHORUS.
Come, we pray, come, O come to-day, Be a worker for the Lord, Be a worker for the Lord;
Heed the call that comes to all, O be a willing worker for the Lord.
Copyright, 1892, by Jno. R. Sweney.

The Lily of the Valley.

English Melody, arranged

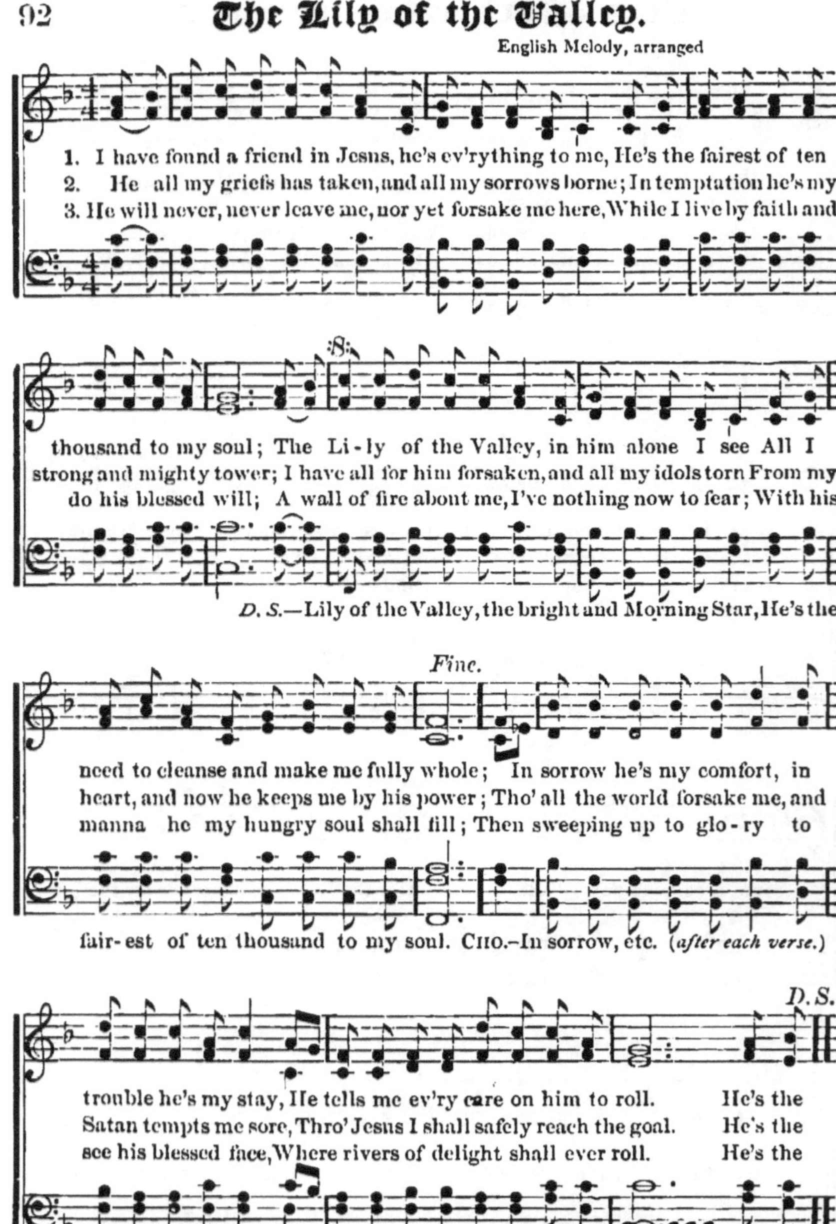
1. I have found a friend in Jesus, he's ev'rything to me, He's the fairest of ten
2. He all my griefs has taken, and all my sorrows borne; In temptation he's my
3. He will never, never leave me, nor yet forsake me here, While I live by faith and
thousand to my soul; The Li - ly of the Valley, in him alone I see All I
strong and mighty tower; I have all for him forsaken, and all my idols torn From my
do his blessed will; A wall of fire about me, I've nothing now to fear; With his
D. S.—Lily of the Valley, the bright and Morning Star, He's the
Fine.
need to cleanse and make me fully whole; In sorrow he's my comfort, in
heart, and now he keeps me by his power; Tho' all the world forsake me, and
manna he my hungry soul shall fill; Then sweeping up to glo - ry to
fair- est of ten thousand to my soul. CHO.–In sorrow, etc. (after each verse.)
D. S.
trouble he's my stay, He tells me ev'ry care on him to roll. He's the
Satan tempts me sore, Thro' Jesus I shall safely reach the goal. He's the
see his blessed face, Where rivers of delight shall ever roll. He's the

Whiter than Snow.

"Wash me, and I shall be whiter than snow."
Psalm li. 7.

JAMES NICHOLSON. WM. G. FISCHER. By per.

1. Lord Je-sus, I long to be per-fect-ly whole; I want thee for-ev-er, to live in my soul; Break down ev-'ry i-dol, cast out ev-'ry foe; Now wash me, and I shall be whit-er than snow.
2. Lord Je-sus, look down from thy throne in the skies, And help me to make a com-plete sac-ri-fice; I give up my-self, and what-ev-er I know—Now wash me, and I shall be whit-er than snow.
3. Lord Je-sus, for this I most humbly en-treat; I wait, blessed Lord, at thy cru-ci-fied feet, By faith, for my cleansing, I see thy blood flow—Now wash me, and I shall be whit-er than snow.
4. Lord Je-sus, thou se-est I pa-tient-ly wait; Come now, and with in me a new heart cre-ate; To those who have sought thee, thou nev-er said'st No—Now wash me, and I shall be whit-er than snow.
CHORUS.
Whiter than snow, yes, whiter than snow;
Now wash me, and I shall be whiter than snow.

Happy Little Workers.

Priscilla J. Owens.
Wm. J. Kirkpatrick.
1. Je - sus is the children's Friend, Happy little workers we; In his love our days we spend, Happy little workers we. Round his throne we love to bend, On his words with joy attend, Je- sus is the children's Friend,
2. Je - sus is the children's King, Happy little workers we; To his mighty hand we cling, Happy little workers we. To his cross our hearts we bring, To his praise our hymns we sing, Je- sus is the children's King,
3. Je - sus is the children's Joy, Happy little workers we; Helping ev - 'ry girl and boy, Happy little workers we. All of e - vil to destroy; May his work our lives employ; Je- sus is the children's Joy,
Happy lit - tle workers we.
Fine. CHORUS.
Happy lit - tle workers, Happy lit - tle workers, Happy little workers we; Serving Je - sus ev - 'ry day,
D.S.
Copyright, 1887, by John J. Hood.

Firm to the End.

JENNIE JOHNSON. JNO. R. SWENEY.

1. We are band - ed togeth - er for Je - sus still to live, And to
2. We are marching togeth - er a- long the bless-ed way Our Re -
3. We are marching togeth - er, sore conflicts we shall meet, But the
4. We are marching togeth - er beyond these fad- ing skies, We are

fol- low wherev- er he may lead; And the grace he has promised we
deemer commandeth us to go; With the cloud and the pil- lar to
Saviour beholds us from his throne; With the sword of the Spir- it temp-
looking beyond the billow's foam; We are wait- ing and watching with

D.S.—tried and the faithful, who

know that he will give If, be - liev - ing, his precious name we plead.
lead us night and day, While be- side us the liv- ing wa- ters flow.
ta- tions we'll defeat, Our pro- tect - or will leave us not a - lone.
calm and trus - ty eyes, Till the Sa- viour shall come and call us home.

Fine.

serve the Master here, Shall be jew - els to sparkle in his crown.

REFRAIN.

Then be firm to the end, then be firm to the end; Let us

never, nev- er lay our ar- mor down, ar - mor down, For the

D.S.

Lead Them to the Light.

Mrs. R. N. Turner. Alt.
Wm. J. Kirkpatrick.
1. There are thousands waiting, waiting for a message from the Lord,
2. They are call- ing," come and help us, lead us from the gloom of night,
3. Tell them that the bless- ed Mas - ter sends his ho - ly, lov- ing word,
4. There are thousands waiting, waiting for the light that shines from heav'n,
Wait- ing for the light of God; In the far off land of
Lead us to the light of God; Lead us to the Sun of
Hast - en with the light of God; O - ver sea and o - ver
Hast - en with the light of God; Send it forth and send it
darkness they are waiting for the light, Waiting for the light of God.
heav- en give us light, O give us light, Lead us to the light of God."
mountains let the joy- ful news be heard, Hasten with the light of God.
glad - ly, free- ly, free - ly was it given, Hasten with the light of God.
CHORUS.
Tell them that it shineth bright, Shines for one and all; Tell them that its blessed rays
Over them shall fall; Tell them, lead them, Lead them to the light of God.
p

Keep the Banner Flying.

Rev. RICHARD OSBORNE.
Rev. ROBERT LOWRY. By per.
1. Keep the banner fly - ing. This our cry shall be, Man - y souls are
2. Keep the bann.r fly - ing; When the faithful fall, Give not up to
3. Keep the banner fly - ing; Christians should agree, With each other
4. Keep the banner fly - ing, O - ver land and sea; By our self-de-
dy - ing, Je - sus must they see; Un - der con- dem- na - tion,
sigh - ing, Christ is all in all; Ral - ly all our forc - es,
vy - ing, Yet in har - mo - ny; Working still for Je - sus,
ny - ing Comes the vic - to - ry; Brighten toil with singing,
Life will soon be gone; On - ly is sal- vation In the Sinless One.
See, the Captain's near; Trust to his resources, There is naught to fear.
Righting human wrong, Till the angels greet us With their welcome song.
Better days will come; To the Saviour clinging, We shall rest at home.
CHORUS.
Shout, shout the bat- tle cry, Girt with endeav - or; Lift, lift the
1st.
2d.
ritard.
banner high, Now and for - ev - er. banner high, Now and forev - er.

Carry the Sunshine.

Fanny L. Jones.
Jno. R. Sweney.
DUET.
1. Car- ry the sunshine with us, While cheeri- ly on we go;
2. Car- ry the sunshine with us, And follow our Lord's command;
3. Car- ry the sunshine with us, To those that have missed it long;
4. Car- ry the sunshine with us In all that we do and say;
Strong in our youthful vig - or, The seed of the word to sow.
Work while the daylight ling - ers, And work with a tire- less hand.
Whisper the name of Je - sus, And tell of his love in song.
Lift from the heart its bur - den, And banish the clouds a - way.
CHORUS.
Car- ry the sunshine, carry the sunshine, Scatter its beams a - round;
Then shall we see, with gladness, The fruitage of grace a - bound.

Praise Him.

Miss M. A. Baker. H. R. Palmer. By per.

1. Praise the Saviour, O ye people! Praise and bless his ho - ly name!
2. Praise him for his mighty actions; Praise him for his ten - derness,
Praise and worship him; children, worship him, For a child from heav'n he came;
When he loving-ly held the lit - tle ones In his arms to save and bless;
Praise him from the hills and mountains, From the vales and cities
Praise him, all ye wise and no- ble, Men and maid - ens, old and
Cho.–Praise him in the sanctu - a - ry; Let the chil - dren swell the
all; Hail him king of earth and heav - en, Who was once a child so
young; Let redeem - ing love and mer - cy Be the theme of ev - 'ry
strain, And at morn, and noon and e - ven, Echo still the sweet re-
D.S. Fine.
small; Hail him king of earth and heaven, Who was once a child so small.
tongue; Let redeem - ing love and mercy Be the theme of ev'ry tongue.
frain; And at morn, and noon and e - ven, Echo still the sweet refrain.

Satisfy us Early.

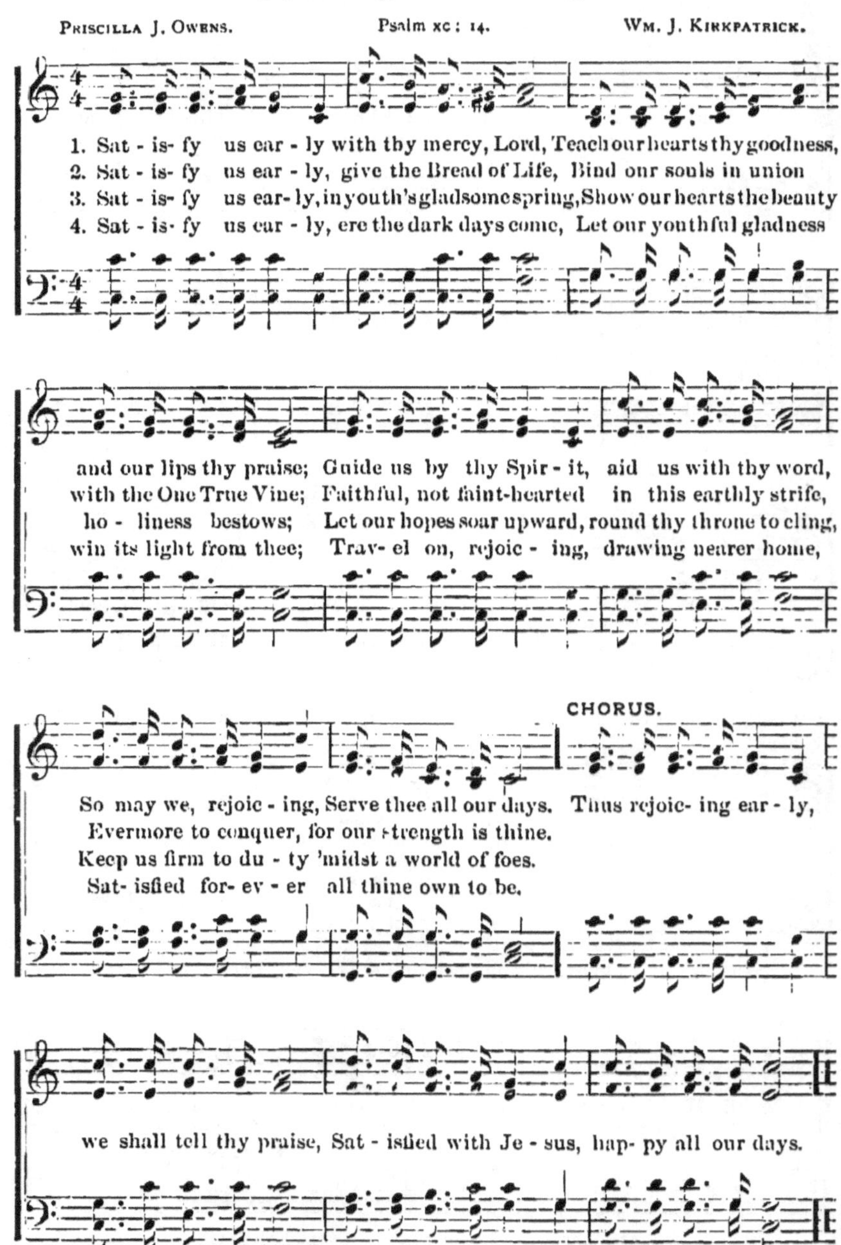
Priscilla J. Owens.
Psalm xc: 14.
Wm. J. Kirkpatrick.
1. Sat - is- fy us ear - ly with thy mercy, Lord, Teach our hearts thy goodness,
2. Sat - is- fy us ear - ly, give the Bread of Life, Bind our souls in union
3. Sat - is- fy us ear- ly, in youth's gladsome spring, Show our hearts the beauty
4. Sat - is- fy us ear - ly, ere the dark days come, Let our youthful gladness
and our lips thy praise; Guide us by thy Spir - it, aid us with thy word,
with the One True Vine; Faithful, not faint-hearted in this earthly strife,
ho - liness bestows; Let our hopes soar upward, round thy throne to cling,
win its light from thee; Trav- el on, rejoic - ing, drawing nearer home,
So may we, rejoic - ing, Serve thee all our days.
Evermore to conquer, for our strength is thine.
Keep us firm to du - ty 'midst a world of foes.
Sat- isfied for- ev - er all thine own to be.
CHORUS.
Thus rejoic- ing ear - ly,
we shall tell thy praise, Sat - isfied with Je - sus, hap- py all our days.
Copyright, 1892, by Wm. J. Kirkpatrick.

He Shall Feed His Flock.

ELIZABETH STILLWELL.
Isa. xl: 11.
JOHN J. HOOD.
1. We will sing you a beau - ti - ful sto - ry, In sweet Bi - ble
2. O Je - sus, our mer - ci - ful Shep - herd, We hear thy soft
3. We will drink of the clear, springing fountains, And rest in the
words it is told, Of Je - sus, the mer - ci - ful Shepherd, Who
call - ing to - day; Lead us in thy fair, blooming pas - ture, And
arms of his love, Till Je - sus, dear Saviour, shall guide us To
welcomes the lambs to his fold.
keep us from wand'ring a - way.
ev - er-green pastures a - bove.
REFRAIN.
He shall feed his flock like a
Shep - herd, And gath - er the lambs with his arm; He shall
car - ry them in his bos - om, And tender - ly shield them from harm.
Copyright, 1892, by John J. Hood.

Keep Your Colors Flying.

"Set up a standard in the land."—Jer. li: 27.

Rev. J. E. Rankin, D. D. Rev. E. S. Lorenz. By per.

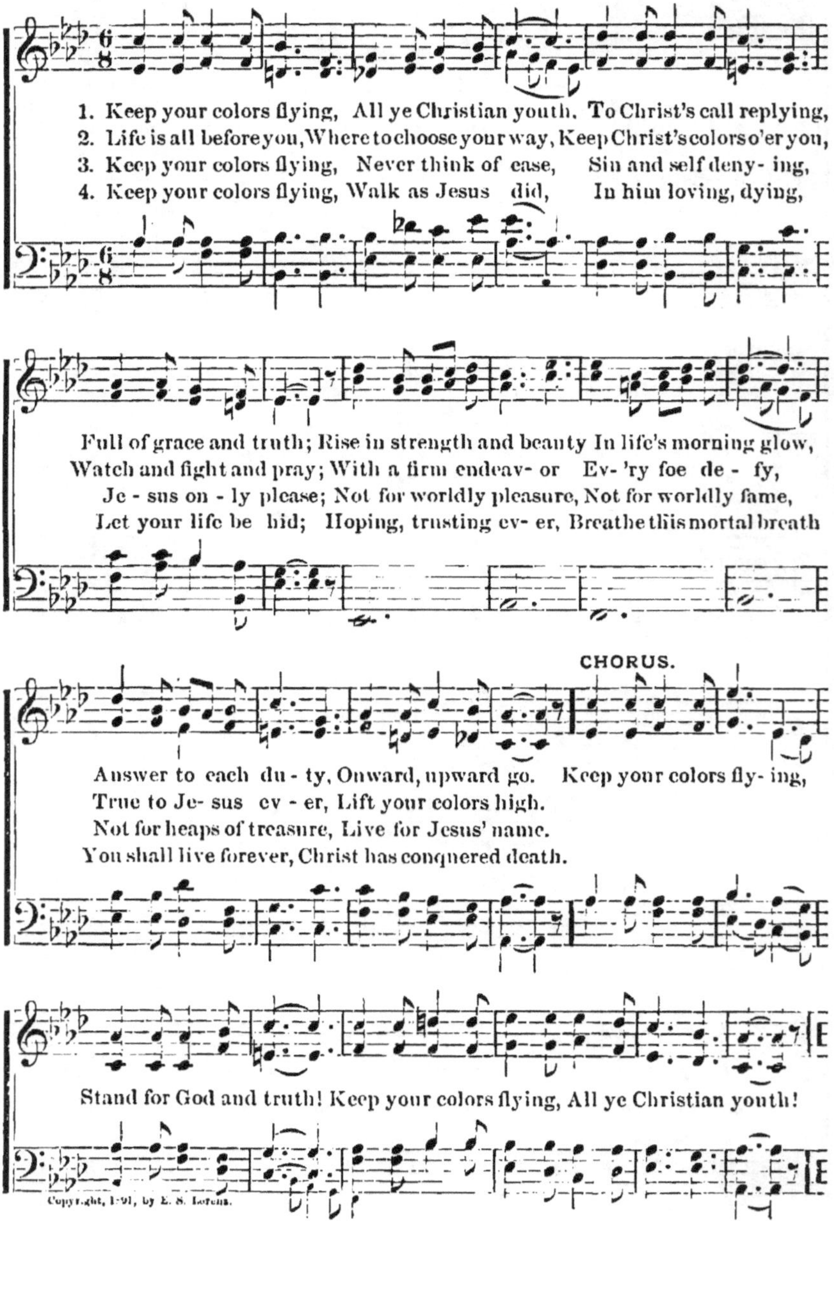

1. Keep your colors flying, All ye Christian youth, To Christ's call replying, Full of grace and truth; Rise in strength and beauty In life's morning glow, Answer to each du- ty, Onward, upward go.
2. Life is all before you, Where to choose your way, Keep Christ's colors o'er you, Watch and fight and pray; With a firm endeav- or Ev- 'ry foe de - fy, True to Je- sus ev - er, Lift your colors high.
3. Keep your colors flying, Never think of ease, Sin and self deny- ing, Je - sus on - ly please; Not for worldly pleasure, Not for worldly fame, Not for heaps of treasure, Live for Jesus' name.
4. Keep your colors flying, Walk as Jesus did, In him loving, dying, Let your life be hid; Hoping, trusting ev- er, Breathe this mortal breath You shall live forever, Christ has conquered death.

CHORUS.

Keep your colors fly- ing, Stand for God and truth! Keep your colors flying, All ye Christian youth!

We've Set Up Our Banner.

"In the name of our Lord we will set up our banner."—Ps. xx: 5.

Mrs. Harriet E. Jones. Jno. R. Sweney.

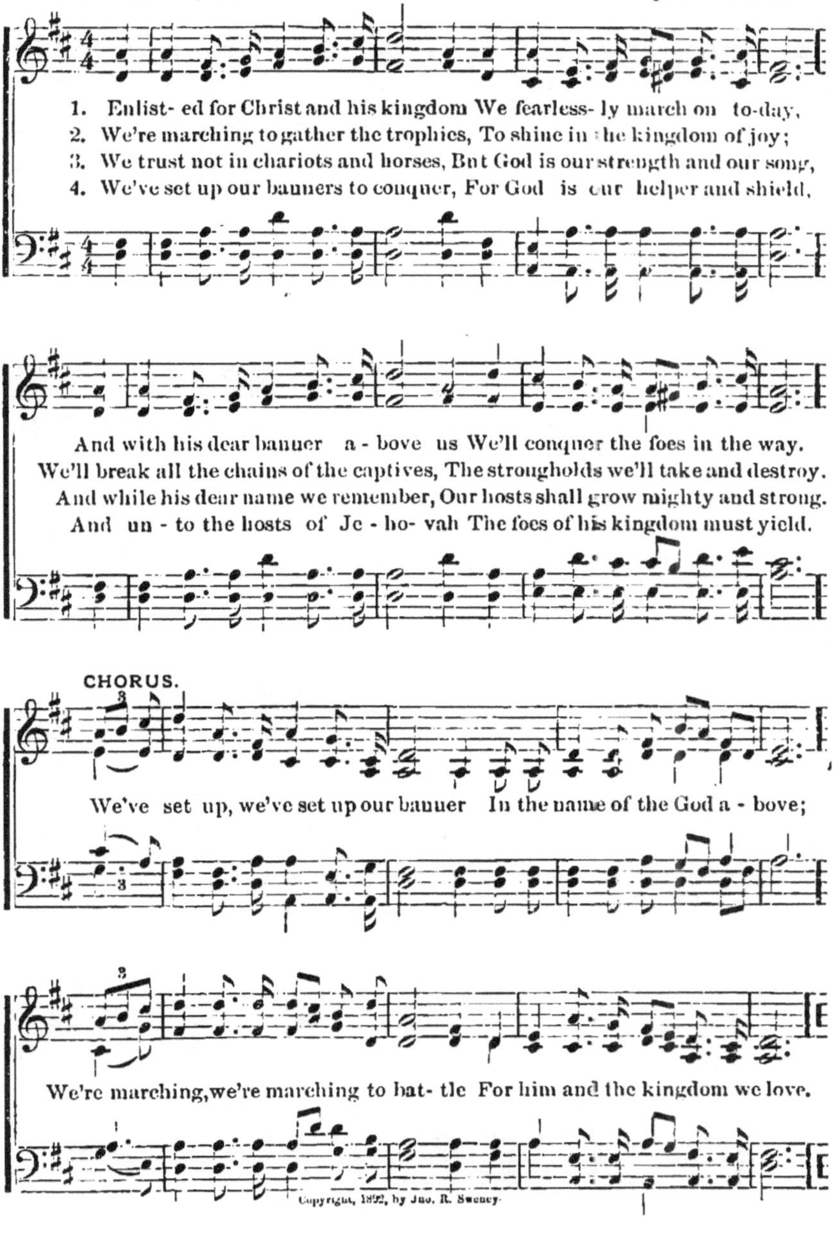

1. Enlist- ed for Christ and his kingdom We fearless- ly march on to-day,
2. We're marching to gather the trophies, To shine in the kingdom of joy;
3. We trust not in chariots and horses, But God is our strength and our song,
4. We've set up our banners to conquer, For God is our helper and shield,

And with his dear banner a - bove us We'll conquer the foes in the way.
We'll break all the chains of the captives, The strongholds we'll take and destroy.
And while his dear name we remember, Our hosts shall grow mighty and strong.
And un - to the hosts of Je - ho - vah The foes of his kingdom must yield.

CHORUS.

We've set up, we've set up our banner In the name of the God a - bove;
We're marching, we're marching to bat- tle For him and the kingdom we love.

Keeping Step Together.

E. E. Hewitt.
Wm. J. Kirkpatrick.
1. Keeping step together In the cause we love, In the happy service Of the King a - bove; May he make us faithful, To his orders true, All that he appoints us Striving still to do.
2. Keeping step together On the King's highway, In the help of Jesus Trusting day by day; May the grace he's promised Freely to bestow Strengthen us for du- ty, Lead us as we go.
3. Keeping step together, Joining heart and hand, All the ranks united Make a might- y band; Helping one another, Working while we sing, May our life-en- deavor Glori - fy our King.
CHORUS.
Keeping step together, Marching on, marching on; Keeping step to- geth- er, Marching on, marching on; Keeping step to- gether In the cause we love, Singing joyful praises To the King a - bove.
Copyright, 1892, by Wm. J. Kirkpatrick.

Gladly will We Sing for Jesus.

Rev. A. Flamman. "Serve the Lord with gladness."—Ps. c: 2. John J. Hood.

1. Glad - ly will we sing for Je - sus, Sing our hap - py songs;
2. Glad - ly will we live for Je - sus, All our earth- ly days;
3. Glad - ly will we die in Je - sus, Lean- ing on his breast;
Prais - es will we give to Je - sus, With our youthful tongues:
Give ourselves en - tire - ly to him, Learn his ho - ly ways:
With his lov - ing arms a - round us, Sweet will be our rest:
Our ho - san- nas loud shall ech - o O - ver sea and land;
Ev - en from our ear - ly child - hood Till our life here ends,
Then we'll ev - er be with Je - sus, With that hap - py throng,
Je - sus is the Friend of chil - dren,— Leads us by the hand.
Will we try to love and serve him, Foll'wing his commands.
Mingling in the heav'nly cho - rus Our triumphant song.
Fine.
D.S.—Ev- er will we own our Sa- viour, And sing our songs of praise.
CHORUS.
Ev - er will we own our Sa - viour, And walk in all his ways;
D.S.

What will You do?

F. G. Burroughs. Adam Geibel.

1. What will you do with the King called Je - sus? Ma - ny are waiting to
2. What will you do for the King called Je - sus, He who for you left his
3. What will you do with the King called Je - sus,—Who will submit to his
hear you say,—Some have despised him, reject- ing his mercy, What will you
throne a - bove, Here 'mid the low - ly and sin - ful to la - bor, Dai - ly un-
gentle sway? Where are the hearts ready now to enthrone him? Who will his
do with your King to-day? What can you witness concerning his goodness,
folding his Father's love. Look on the fields white already to harvest,
kind commands o - bey? Come with your ointments most costly and precious,
Who died to save you from sin's bitter thrall? Who will declare him the
Who now is willing to toil with the few? What will you do for the
Pour out your gifts at the dear Saviour's feet: Ren - der to him all your
fair - est of thousands? Who now will crown him the Lord of all?
dear Saviour, Je - sus? Lo, he is wait - ing, he calls for you!
loy - al de - vo - tion; Seek to ex - alt him by prais - es meet.

CHORUS. *Voices in unison.*

What will you do with the King called Jesus? What, oh, what will you do with Jesus?

Voices in parts.

He waits to bless all who humbly confess Faith in his blood and righteousness.

Into Thy Keeping.

FANNY J. CROSBY. JNO R. SWENEY.

1. Into thy keeping our hearts we give, Je- sus our blessed Redeem - er;
2. Help us to la- bor with earnest love, Je- sus our blessed Redeem - er;
3. Patient and faithful we long to be, Je- sus our blessed Redeem - er;
4. Help us to honor and do thy will, Je- sus our blessed Redeem - er;

Fine.

Help us to promise for thee to live, Je- sus our Lord and King.
Gather- ing souls for thy fold a- bove, Je- sus our Lord and King.
Willing to spend and be spent for thee, Je- sus our Lord and King.
May we our du- ties with joy ful - fill, Je- sus our Lord and King.

D.S.—Careful in all that we do and say, Je- sus our Lord and King.

CHORUS. *D.S.*

Grant us the light of thy grace to-day, Teach us to walk in the heav'nly way.

The Endeavor Band.
L. F. Lindsay.
Jno. R. Sweney.
Moderato.
1. A Christian band . . . . from far and near, ... We meet to learn . . . of Jesus here, . . . To read his word, . . whose ev'ry line . . . . Is full of hope . . . and joy di - vine. . . .
2. A Christian band . . . where all may sing . . . Glad songs of praise . . . to God our King, . . And youthful hearts . . may find the way . . . . To perfect peace . . . and endless day. . . .
3. Each willing hand . . . and thankful heart . . . . Is bound a-gain . . . before we part, . . As sheaves on earth . are bound with twine, . . . His word shall bind . . . as cords divine. . .
4. The Master's work . . . . we'll still pursue, ... And once a-gain . . . our pledge renew, . . . To him who saves . . . us by his love, ... Till gathered home . . . with him a- bove. . . .
CHORUS.
This blest Endeavor band, All o'er this broad, bright land, Is gathered in his name, To grasp the friendly hand; Our thoughts are one in thee, Our
Copyright, 1889, 1890, by Jno. R. Sweney.

prayers will ever be, That God may bless and keep The Y. P. S. C. E.

Our Sunday School *Music above.*

1 Our Sunday-school, how sweet, how dear
To meet and learn of Jesus here;
To read his word, whose ev'ry line
Is full of hope and joy divine.

Cho.—Our blessed Sunday-school,
Our bright and happy home,
Within thy peaceful dome
We love, we love to come:
Our thoughts will cling to thee,
And still our prayer will be,
That God may bless and keep our
Sunday-school.

2 Our Sunday-school, where all may sing
Glad songs of praise to God our King,
And youthful hearts may find the way
To perfect peace and endless day.

3 Our school is like a garden fair,
Where plants are trained with tender care
To bloom for him, the Lord of all,
Whose loving smiles like sunbeams fall.

4 Our Sunday-school, whose golden hours
From Eden bring refreshing showers,
In thee on earth we learn to live,
For thee our thanks to God we give.

Gentle Saviour, Bend Thine Ear.

E. E. Hewitt. Jno. R. Sweney.

1. Gentle Saviour, bend thine ear, Hear our pray'r, hear our pray'r; Thou art always
D.S.—Guide us, tender
Fine.
CHORUS.
ver - y near, Keep us in thy care. May we nes- tle by thy side,
Shepherd, guide, To thy pastures fair.

D.S.
Hap- py in thy love abide;

2 Gentle Saviour, we have strayed
From thy way, from thy way,
Thy kind voice have disobeyed,
Pardon us to-day.

3 Gentle Saviour, thou didst die
"Once for all," "once for all,"
Thou art living now on high,
Hear the children call.

Rally for the Master.

E. E. Hewitt.
Wm. J. Kirkpatrick.
VOICES IN UNISON.
1. Rally for the Master, Soldiers brave and true, Keep his blood-stain'd banner
2. Rally for the Master, Give the countersign, Shout aloud the watchword,
3. Rally for the Master, For the cause we love; Crown his name with blessing,
Ev- er in full view; In the Christian warfare Take a valiant stand,
Pass it down the line! Christ, our Lord and Saviour, And the Church he bought,
Name all names above! By his word and Spir- it Conquer in the fight,
In this work for Jesus, Come, and lend a hand.
Claim our glad allegiance, Love, and time, and thought.
Take the world for Jesus, Glory to his might!
CHORUS.
Rally, rally, Comrades, true and faithful, Rally, rally, For the blessed King; Soldiers of "Endeavor,"
Com- rades, com- rades, true and faith - ful, Comrades, rally for the bless - ed King;
We are his for- ev - er, Let us falter never, Ral- ly for our King.
Copyright, 1892, by Wm. J. Kirkpatrick.

A Royal Army.

C. H. G. — Chas. H. Gabriel.

1. A roy- al ar - my, marching Against the pow'rs of wrong, of wrong, As
2. A mighty ar- my, faith- ful Each soldier, brave and true, and true, We
3. A valiant christian ar - my, For right we bravely stand; we stand, Our

loy- al as the sunbeams, We sing our bat- tle song; En-list - ed for the
ral- ly round the standard, And on our way pursue; We have no cause for
vic- to - ry is cer- tain, For Jesus has command; "Up, onward" is our

con - flict We proudly march and sing, we sing, Our cause the cause of
doubt- ing, The way is full of cheer, of cheer, Our Captain is be-
mot - to: We do not fear the foe, the foe, The crown is just be-

CHORUS.

Je - sus,—Hosanna to our King. March - ing on - ward, ev - - er
fore us, We have no need to fear.
fore us,—Rejoicing on we go. Marching on, Marching on, Marching onward,

on - ward, With a song we press a- long, In the service of our King.
ev - er on- ward,

Words of Jesus.

E. E. Hewitt. Wm. J. Kirkpatrick.

Matt. xi. 28. 1. Come unto me, the Saviour said, Come unto me, the Saviour said;
John xiv 6. 2. I am the way, the truth, the life, I am the way, the truth, the life;
Mark x. 21. 3. Take up the cross, and follow me, Take up the cross, and follow me;
Matt. vii. 7 4. Ask and it shall be given you, Ask and it shall be given you;
Come unto me, the Saviour said, And I will give you rest.
I am the way, the truth, the life, I am the light of the world. John viii. 12.
Take up the cross, and fol - low me, And thou shalt have treasure in heaven.
Ask and it shall be giv - en you, Seek and ye shall find.
CHORUS.
Oh, the blessed words of Je - sus! Precious words! hallowed words!
Oh, the blessed words of Je - sus! Words of life to me.

John iii. 36.
5 He that believeth | on the Son, :||
Hath everlasting | life.

Is. xlv. 22.
6 Look unto me, and | be ye saved, :||
All the ends of the | earth.

Matt. v. 8.
7 Blessed are the | pure in heart, :||
For | they shall see | God.

Matt v. 12.
8 Re- | joice and be ex- | ceeding glad, :||
For | great is your reward in | heaven.

John xiv. 18.
9 I | will not leave you | comfortless, ||
I will come unto | you.

John vii. 37.
10 If | any man thirst let him | come unto [me, :||
And drink of the water of | life.

Mark. x. 14.
11 Suffer little children to | come unto me. :||
For of | such is the kingdom of | [heaven.

John xiv. 2.
12 I | go to prepare a | place for you, ||
In my Fathers' house.

Because He Loves Me So.

Rev. E. A. Hoffman. Gabriel Miesse.

1. Why came the Saviour from a - bove, To dwell on earth be - low?
Why suffered he on Cal - va - ry? Because he loves me so.

2. Why bowed he in Gethsem - a - ne Be- neath a weight of woe,
Till blood- y sweat bedew'd the ground? Because he loves me so.

3. Why does he wash my sin-stained heart And make it white as snow?
Why does he make his home therein? Because he loves me so.

4. Why will he take me up to heav'n From cares and toils be - low?
Why give a crown of glo - ry there? Because he loves me so.

CHORUS.

He loves me, he loves me, He loves me, this I know,
He loves, he loves me, He loves, he loves me, this I know,
He gave himself to die for me, Because he loves me so.

Arr. from "Happy Songs," by per.

Marching On, Rejoicing.

E. E. Hewitt. Wm. J. Kirkpatrick.

1. Marching on, re - joic- ing, Happy songs ascend; Many voices mingle, Many praises blend; We are serving Je - sus, His Endeavor Band; By his grace he's call'd us, In his name we stand.
2. Marching on, re - joic- ing, In life's morning hour, On his help rely- ing, Trusting in his power; Ev - er pressing on- ward, Lift the standard high, Stepping upward daily, Follow to the sky.
3. Marching on, rejoicing, Those who've gone before, Looking down from glory, Call us ev- er - more; Ours is now the bat - tle, Now the course we run; Blessed Saviour, keep us Till the crown is won.

CHORUS.

Marching on, rejoicing, Marching on, marching on; Marching on, rejoicing, Happy songs as- cend; Marching on, re- joicing, Marching on, marching on; Many voices mingle, Many praises blend.

We Will.

FANNY J. CROSBY. JNO. R. SWENEY.

1. 'Tis thy command that ev - 'ry one Should thy dis - ci - ple be,
2. 'Tis thy command that ev - 'ry heart Thy temple, Lord, should be,
3. 'Tis thy command that we should grow In grace from day to day,
4. And since o - be - dience to thy law Our test of love must be,
'Tis thy command that we should leave Our all, and fol - low thee.
Should keep the per - fect law of love, And walk by faith with thee.
Should watch against the tempter's power, And not for - get to pray.
Ac - cept the wil - ling sac - ri - fice That now we bring to thee.
CHORUS.
'Tis thy command, with heart and hand
Thy cause de- fend - ing still, To do and dare,
thy cross to bear; And by thy grace we will.

Jesus Saves.

Priscilla J. Owens.
Wm. J. Kirkpatrick.
1. We have heard a joy - ful sound, Je - sus saves, Je - sus saves;
2. Waft it on the roll - ing tide, Je - sus saves, Je - sus saves;
3. Sing a - bove the bat - tle's strife, Je - sus saves, Je - sus saves;
4. Give the winds a might - y voice, Je - sus saves, Je - sus saves;
Spread the glad - ness all a - round, Je - sus saves, Je - sus saves;
Tell to sin - ners, far and wide, Je - sus saves, Je - sus saves;
By his death and end - less life, Je - sus saves, Je - sus saves;
Let the na - tions now re - joice, Je - sus saves, Je - sus saves;
Bear the news to ev' - ry land, Climb the steeps and cross the waves.
Sing, ye is - lands of the sea, E - cho back, ye o - cean caves,
Sing it soft - ly thro' the gloom, When the heart for mer - cy craves,
Shout sal - va - tion full and free, High - est hills and deepest caves,
Onward, 'tis our Lord's command, Je - sus saves, Je - sus saves.
Earth shall keep her ju - bi - lee, Je - sus saves, Je - sus saves.
Sing in tri - umph o'er the tomb, Je - sus saves, Je - sus saves.
This our song of vic - to - ry, Je - sus saves, Je - sus saves.

Keep Step.

S. Martin.
Wm. J. Kirkpatrick.
1. Keep step, keep step to the army tread, By the Lord of hosts our Commander led;
2. Keep step, keep step, let our hearts rejoice,
Till we hear the sound of our Leader's voice;
3. Keep step, keep step to the joyful song Of the angel choir, as we march along;
4. Keep step, keep step till our feet shall stand At the pearly gates of the morning land;
Keep step, keep step with the ranks we fill, Let us all march on, and be faithful still.
Keep step, keep step where he bids us go, To the battle front, and defeat the foe.
Keep step, keep step while their glad harps ring,
And they praise the name of the Lord our King.
Keep step, keep step till we enter there, And forget our toil in the bliss we share.
CHORUS.
Keep step, keep step, Keep step till the march of life is done; Keep step, keep
Keep step, keep step, Keep step,
step, Till the victor-crown is won.
keep step,
INTERLUDE.
Copyright, 189?, by Wm. J. Kirkpatrick.

Go and Speak to Others.

Fanny J. Crosby.
Jno. R. Sweney.
1. Go and speak to others Loving words and true, That is what our Saviour Tells us we must do; If his steps to fol - low All of us a - gree, Oh, how light and happy Will our toiling be.
2. Do - ing good to others, Let us now be - gin, To our Junior meeting Bring the children in; Treat them ver - y kind - ly, Make them feel at home, Then to join our number They will gladly come.
3. Do - ing good to others, Helping all around, In the path of du - ty May we all be found, Singing like the spring birds In their mer - ry glee, Shining like the sunbeams Ev'ry one can see.
CHORUS.
Look up, lift up, list - en to the call, Look up, lift up, give a hand to all; Lift up the wea - ry one, say to those oppressed, Come to our Redeem - er, he will give you rest.

Let us Give our Youth to Jesus.
L. H. Edmunds.
Wm. J. Kirkpatrick.
Duet or Quartet.
1. Let us give our youth to Je - sus, Bring the brightest, sweetest hours,
2. Let us serve our King with gladness, And his wondrous love proclaim,
3. Let us bring our as - pir - a - tions, All that we would be and do,
4. Let us give our youth to Je - sus, Ere the shadows gath - er dim,
Ere the sunbeams lose their spar - kle, Ere the dew has left the flow'rs.
He will bless the lips' "en-deav-or," Bless the deed wrought "in his name."
To the One whose grace can make us No - ble - heart - ed, pure and true.
Hap - py is the life, and bless - ed, Whol - ly yield - ed un - to him.
Chorus.
While the skies o'erflow With the morning glow, Let us come to Jesus now.
While our hearts are gay, In life's blooming May, Let us come to Jesus now.
Let us come, let us come, Let us come to Je - sus now!
let us come, let us come,
Copyright, 1890, by Wm. J. Kirkpatrick.

We are Singing On the Way.

L. H. EDMUNDS. CHAS. EDW. POLLOCK.

1. We are sing - ing on the way, To a blessed land of day, Where the
2. What though trials here we meet? Soon we'll walk the golden street, Where we'll
3. We are pressing on the way, Let us work, and watch, and pray, Winning
raptured hal - le - lu - jahs nev - er cease; We will see its shining towers,
look up - on the beau - ty of our King; Tears of sorrow here may flow,
stars to sparkle in our crowns of light; Let us tell the Saviour's love,
Fine.
Rest within its lovely bowers, In that Eden-land of ev- er- lasting peace.
But "hereafter we shall know," And redeeming love thro' endless ages sing.
Till he bids us come above, Where no shadow ever mars the radiance bright.
D.S.—glory we shall share, In the house of "many mansions," bright and fair.
CHORUS.
Blessed home! blessed home! In the house of "many
Blessed home! blessed home!
mansions," bright and fair; For we'll be like Je- sus there, And his
bright and fair;
D.S.

Up and Away.

Fanny J. Crosby.
Jno. R. Sweney.
1. Heard ye the voice of the Master call? Up and a- way, up and a- way;
2. Work for the cause that we love so dear, Up and a- way, up and a- way;
3. Trust in the Lord while the seed we sow, Up and a- way, up and a- way;
4. Work with a will, let us faithful be, Up and a- way, up and a- way;
Out in the field there's a place for all, Up and away, a - way.
Toil will be sweet with the Saviour near, Up and away, a - way.
Trust in the Lord and the fruit will grow, Up and away, a - way.
Then what a reaping we all may see, Up and away, a - way.
CHORUS.
Work while the spring of our youth is bright,
Work while our hearts and our steps are light,
Work from the morn to the calm, still night, Up and away, a - way.

Stepping-stones to Jesus.

E. E. Hewitt. Wm. J. Kirkpatrick.

Moderato.
1. Stepping-stones to Je-sus All our joys may be, Used with glad thanksgiving
2. Stepping-stones to Je-sus, Leading to his feet, Are the lit-tle tri-als,
3. Stepping-stones to Je-sus, All the pure delight In his works of beauty,
4. Stepping-stones to Jesus, Blessed means of grace; Prayer and sweet communion
For his love so free. Many, many blessings In our pathway fall, Stepping-stones to
Which we daily meet; Ev'ry need that presses, Ev'ry vexing care, Ev'ry dis-ap-
All things fair and bright. Ev'ry sweet affection, Tender human love, Brought in conse-
In the sacred place; Ev'ry self-denial For the Master's cause, Each renewed o-
CHORUS.
Jesus We may find them all. Looking for the stepping-stones
pointment, Ev'ry cross we bear. Placed along life's way;
cration To the Friend above.
beying Of his ho-ly laws.
Looking for the stepping-stones, We find them ev'ry day; Stepping-stones to Jesus,
p
poco rit.
ad lib.
Stepping-stones to Jesus, Looking for the stepping-stones, We find them ev'ry day.

Lead Me, Saviour.

F. M. D.
"For thy name's sake lead me, guide me"—Ps. xxxi. 3.
FRANK M. DAVIS.
With expression.
1. Saviour, lead me, lest I stray, Gent- ly lead me all the way;
2. Thou the refuge of my soul When life's stormy billows roll,
3. Saviour, lead me, then at last, When the storm of life is past,
1. Sav - iour, lead me, lest I stray, Gent - ly lead me all the way;
I am safe when by thy side, I would in thy love abide.
I am safe when thou art nigh, All my hopes on thee rely.
To the land of endless day, Where all tears are wiped away.
I am safe when by thy side, I would in thy love abide.
CHORUS.
Lead me, lead me, Sav - iour, lead me, lest I stray; . . .
lest I stray;
rit. e dim.
Gently down the stream of time, Lead me, Saviour, all the way.
stream of time,
all the way.
From "Carols of Joy," by per.

Ye Have Done it Unto Me.

L. H. Edmunds. Wm. J. Kirkpatrick.

1. Have you carried cups of water, From the fresh and living spring, To the thirs- ty, faint and wea- ry, For the love of Christ our King? Then, when all the journey's end- ed, Sweet the welcome home will be, When you hear the Master saying, "Ye have done it un - to me,"
2. Have you tried to cheer the stranger? Spoken comfort to the sad? Have you helped the poor and need- y? Made the lit- tle chil-dren glad? Then, be- yond the walls of jas- per, By the shining crys- tal sea, You will
3. Have you brightened lonely pathways With the gentle light of love, And to those who grope in darkness Brought the sunshine from above? When the trumpet has re-sound-ed, For the last great ju - bi - lee, You will
REFRAIN.
Un - to me, un- to me,
ad lib.
{ When you / You will } hear the Master saying,
"Ye have done it unto me."

chil - dren, That Je-sus will help them to do, to do, If they to his
voice will but list - en, And al-ways be faith-ful and true.
The Children's Offering.
Eliza E. Hewitt.
Jno. R. Swenev.
Moderato.
1. Flowers breathe their fragrance, Birds give their song, Stars shine in beau-ty
2. Thoughts pure and ho - ly, Words kind and true, All gen-tle ser - vice,
3. Faith that will trust him, Hope that will smile, Though clouds may cover
All the night long, Voic - es of na - ture Prais - es re - peat;
Lit - tle hands do; Work for our Mas - ter, Joy - ful and sweet,
Blue skies a-while; Hearts that will al - ways With his love beat;
Fine. CHORUS. D.S.
What can the children Lay at his feet? When thro' his mercy Je- sus we meet,
Prayer for his kingdom Lay at his feet.
Children, these treasures Lay at his feet.
Copyright, 1887, by John J. Hood.
D.S.–We will our bright crowns Lay at his feet.

All Hail the Power.

E. Perronett.
Wm. J. Kirkpatrick.
1. All hail the power of Je- sus' name! Let an - gels prostrate fall;
2. Crown him, ye morning stars of light, Who fixed this earthly ball;
3. Ye chos - en seed of Is- rael's race, Ye ransomed from the fall,
4. Sin - ners, whose love can ne'er for - get The wormwood and the gall,
Bring forth the roy - al di - a- dem, And crown him Lord of all.
Now hail the strength of Israel's might, And crown him Lord of all.
Hail him who saves you by his grace, And crown him Lord of all.
Go, spread your tro- phies at his feet, And crown him Lord of all.
And crown him, crown him, Crown him Lord of all; Bring
And crown him, crown him, Crown him Lord of all; Now
And crown him, crown him, Crown him Lord of all; Hail
And crown him, crown him, Crown him Lord of all; Go,
forth the roy - al di - a - dem, And crown him Lord of all.
hail the strength of Israel's might, And crown him Lord of all.
him who saves you by his grace, And crown him Lord of all.
spread your trophies at his feet, And crown him Lord of all.

5 Let every kindred, every tribe,
On this terrestial ball
To him all majesty ascribe,
And crown him Lord of all.

6 O that with yonder sacred throng
We at his feet may fall!
We'll join the everlasting song,
And crown him Lord of all.

Our Father in Heaven.

E. A. Barnes. Jno. R. Sweney.

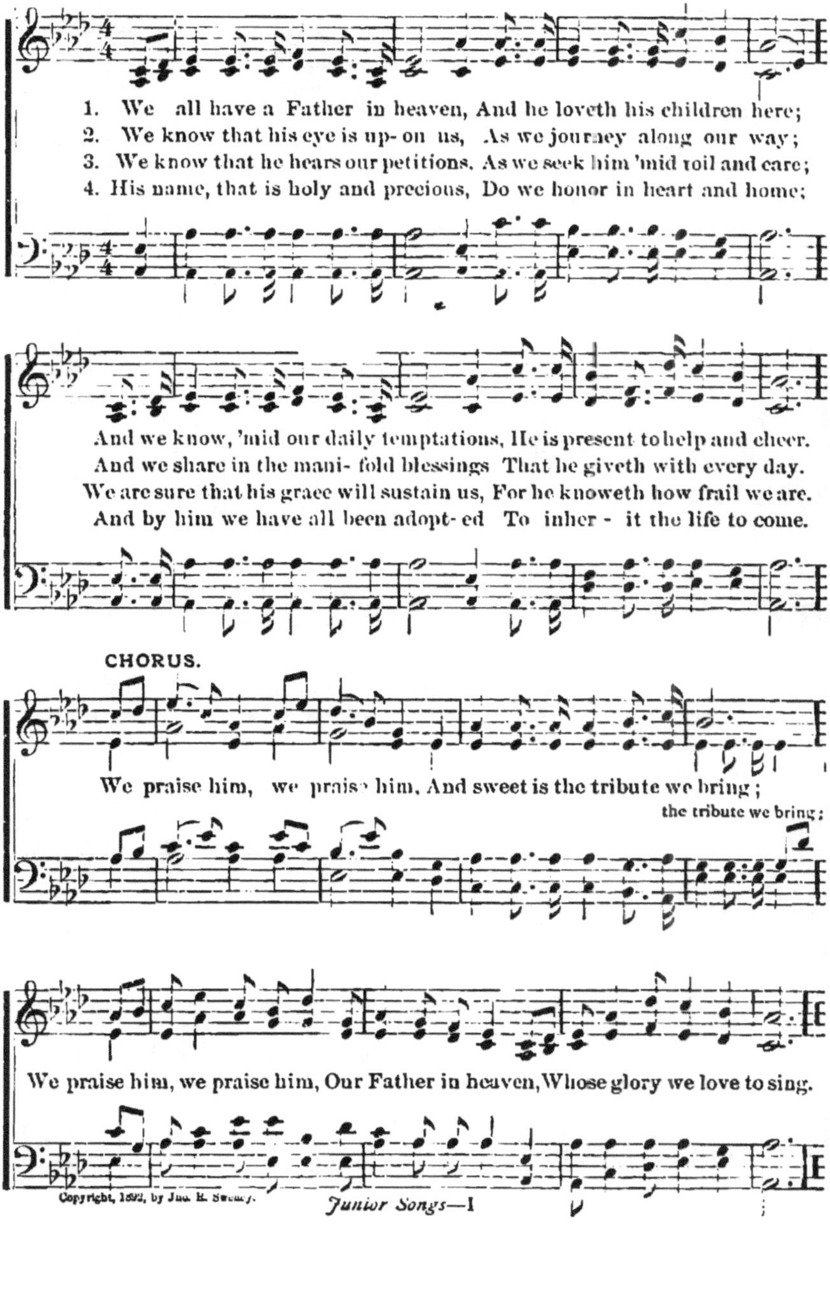

1. We all have a Father in heaven, And he loveth his children here;
2. We know that his eye is up- on us, As we journey along our way;
3. We know that he hears our petitions, As we seek him 'mid toil and care;
4. His name, that is holy and precious, Do we honor in heart and home;

And we know, 'mid our daily temptations, He is present to help and cheer.
And we share in the mani- fold blessings That he giveth with every day.
We are sure that his grace will sustain us, For he knoweth how frail we are.
And by him we have all been adopt- ed To inher - it the life to come.

CHORUS.

We praise him, we praise him, And sweet is the tribute we bring;
the tribute we bring;

We praise him, we praise him, Our Father in heaven, Whose glory we love to sing.

Seeking for Me.

E. E. Hasty.

1. Jesus, my Saviour, to Bethlehem came, Born in a manger to sorrow and shame;
2. Jesus, my Saviour, on Calvary's tree, Paid the great debt, and my soul he set free;
3. Jesus, my Saviour, the same as of old, While I did wander afar from the fold,
4. Jesus, my Saviour, shall come from on high, Sweet is the promise as weary years fly;
Oh, it was wonder- ful, blest be his name, Seeking for me, for me.
Oh, it was wonder- ful, how could it be? Dy - ing for me, for me.
Gent- ly and long he hath pled with my soul, Calling for me, for me.
Oh, I shall see him descending the sky, Coming for me, for me.
for me, ... for me; . . . .
Seeking for me, seeking for me, Seeking for me, seeking for me
Dy-ing for me, dying for me, Dy-ing for me, dying for me;
Call-ing for me, calling for me, Call-ing for me, calling for me:
Com-ing for me, coming for me, Com-ing for me, coming for me,
Oh, it was wonderful, blest be his name, Seeking for me, for me.
Oh, it was wonderful, how could it be? Dy-ing for me, for me.
Gent-ly and long he hath pled with my soul, Calling for me, for me.
Oh, I shall see him descending the sky, Coming for me, for me.
By per. of Towne & Sullivan.

There's a Hand Held Out.

M. W. Morse.
Jno R. Sweney.
1. There's a hand held out in pi- ty, There's a hand held out in love; It will
2. Oh, how gently will it lead us! Oh, how tender is its touch! 'Tis the
3. Yes, 'tis love to me, a sin- ner, Prompts this hand to reach so low, Striving
4. Shall I, to this hand extended, Pay no heed as it in - vites? Shall my
pi - lot to the ci - ty, Where our Father dwells a - bove.
bless - ed hand of Je - sus; We all need it, oh, so much!
thus to be the win - ner, Ere I reap what I shall sow.
Sav - iour be of- fend - ed, Give I not to him his rights?
CHORUS.
There's a hand held out to you, to you, There's a hand held out to me, to me,
There's a hand that will prove true, Whatev - er our lot shall be.
prove true,
Copyright, 188J, by Jno. R. Sweney.

5 Nay, I would this proffered hand take,
Knowing that it leads aright;
Yes, I would this loving choice make;
Trusting in his love and might.

6 Then, as hand in hand together
With my Saviour, with my Friend,
With my Christ, my Elder Brother,
Let him lead till life shall end.

There is a Green Hill.

Jno. R. Sweney.

GIRLS.
1. There is a green hill far a-way, With-out a ci-ty wall,
2. He died that we might be forgiven, He died to make us good,
Where the dear Lord was cru-ci-fied, Who died to save us all.
That we might go at last to hea-ven, Saved by his pre-cious blood.
SOLO—BOYS.
We may not know, we can-not tell, What
There was no oth-er good e-nough To
pains he had to bear, ... But we be-
pay the price of sin; . . . . He on-ly

lieve it was for us He hung and suf - fered there.
could un - lock the gate Of heaven, and let us in.

rit.

SCHOOL.

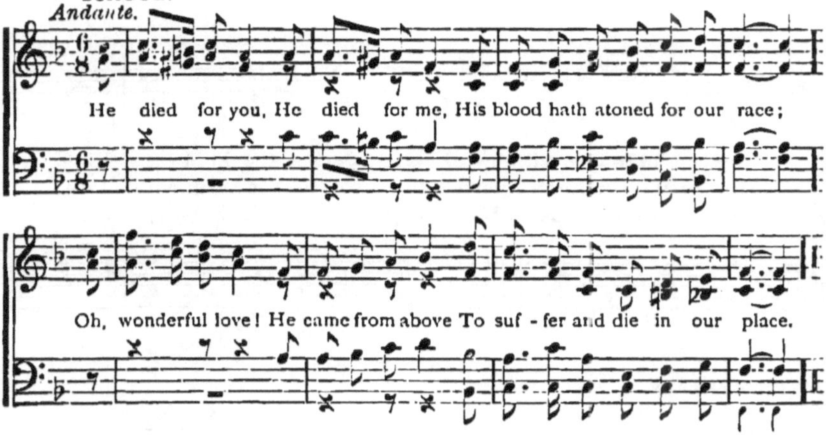

Andante.

He died for you, He died for me, His blood hath atoned for our race;

Oh, wonderful love! He came from above To suf - fer and die in our place.

Doxology.

Words arr. by B. M. A.

{J. R. S.
W. J. K.
J. J. H.

Slow with dignity.

Glory be to the Fa-ther, Glory be to the Son, Glory be to the Holy Ghost;

As it was in the beginning, Is now, and ever shall be, World without end. Amen, amen.

Singing His Praises.

W. L. M. W. L. Mason.

1. Let us u - nite and sing his praise, Je- sus is King, Je- sus is King;
2. He came because he loved me so, Down from above, down from above;
3. He gently leads us ev - 'ry day, Praise to his name, praise to his name;
Crown him in love with joyful lays, Je- sus the Lord is King.
He is the children's Friend, I know, He looks on them with love.
He will be with us all the way, Praise to his ho - ly name.
REFRAIN.
Singing his prais- es, singing his praises, Je - sus, the children's King;
We will rejoice and with hap- py voice, Ev - er his prais- es sing.

We'll Never Say Good By.

"We shall never say 'good by' in heaven."—The words of a dying Christian woman.

Mrs. E. W. Chapman. J. H. Tenney.

1. Our friends on earth we meet with pleasure, While swift the moments fly,
2. How joyful is the thought that lingers, When loved ones cross death's sea,
3. No parting words shall e'er be spoken In that bright land of flowers,
Yet ev - er comes the thought of sadness That we must say good by.
That when our la - bors here are end - ed, With them we'll ev - er be.
But songs of joy, and peace, and gladness, Shall ev - ermore be ours.
CHORUS.
We'll nev - er say good by in heaven, We'll never say good by, . . .
For in that land of joy and song We'll never say good by.
Repeat Chorus pp

Tell Me the Story of Jesus.

FANNY J. CROSBY. JNO. R. SWENEY.

1. Tell me the sto - ry of Je - sus, Write on my heart ev-'ry word,
2. Fasting, a- lone in the des - ert, Tell of the days that he passed,
3. Tell of the cross where they nailed him, Writhing in anguish and pain;
CHO.—Tell me the sto - ry of Je - sus, Write on my heart ev'ry word,
Fine.
Tell me the sto - ry most precious, Sweetest that ev - er was heard;
How for our sins he was tempted, Yet was triumphant at last;
Tell of the grave where they laid him, Tell how he liv - eth a- gain;
Tell me the sto - ry most precious, Sweetest that ev - er was heard.
Tell how the angels, in cho - rus, Sang as they welcomed his birth,—
Tell of the years of his la - bor, Tell of the sorrow he bore,
Love in that sto - ry so ten - der, Clear - er than ev - er I see;
D. C.
Glo - ry to God in the high - est! Peace and good tidings to earth.
He was despised and af-flict - ed, Homeless, reject - ed and poor.
Stay, let me weep while you wisper, Love paid the ransom for me.

Praise God, Eternal King.

E. E. Hewitt.
Wm. J. Kirkpatrick.
1. Oh, praise him! oh, praise him! Praise him, ye children of Zion, E - ternal King, E-
2. Oh, praise him! oh, praise him! Praise him, ye children of Zion, E - ternal King, E-
ternal King! Eternal King! Praise him from the height; Praise him, stars of light; Praise him,
ter- nal King! E-ter-nal King! Praise him, angel band, Who in glory stand; Seraphs
golden beams of day, Turning shadows far a- way. Praise God, ye children of
bright, and cher- ubim, Raise the ev - er-lasting hymn. Praise God, ye children of
2nd time go to Semi-Chorus.
SOLO.
A little slower.
Zi - on, Praise God, e - ter - nal King.
Zi - on, Praise God, e - ter - nal King.
Not the shining host a - lone, . .
And the grateful notes they raise, .
D.C.
Circling 'round the great white throne, But his earthly children sing, Glory to their blessed [King,
Help to swell his endless praise, Meet the songs of joy and love, Ringing from the harps above.

SEMI-CHORUS.
Lift your hearts above, Tell his tender love; Sing, gladly sing;
Praise him with delight, Sing his boundless might. Sing, gladly sing;
Hearts and voices bring, In glo - ry, in glo - ry to the King of
Joy - ful anthems bring, In glo - ry, in glo - ry to the King of
Rit
kings, In glo - ry, in glo - ry to the King of kings.
kings, In glo - ry, in glo - ry to the King of kings.
FULL CHORUS.
While the heav'nly worlds a - dore him, Let our hearts bow down be- fore him;
Send his prais- es ring - ing o - ver land and sea; Send his prais-es ringing o - ver

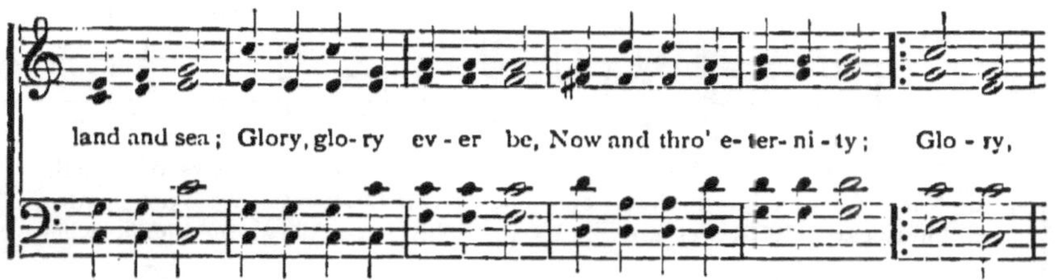
land and sea; Glory, glo- ry ev - er be, Now and thro' e- ter- ni - ty; Glo - ry,

Glo - - ry to the King of kings.
glory, glory to the King of kings. Glory in the highest, glory, Glory to the King of kings.

Responsive Thanksgiving.

J. R. S

LEADER.—O give thanks unto the Lord; for he is good:

RESPONSE

For his mer - cy en - dur - eth for - ev - er.

LEADER.—To him that stretched out the earth above the waters:
RESPONSE.—For his mercy, etc.
LEADER—To him that made great lights:
RESPONSE—For his mercy, etc.
LEADER.—The sun to rule by day: the moon and stars to rule by night;
RESPONSE.—For his mercy, etc.
LEADER.—To him which led his people through the wilderness:
RESPONSE.—For his mercy, etc.
LEADER.—Who remembered us in our low estate:
RESPONSE.—For his mercy, etc.
LEADER.—And hath redeemed us from our enemies:
RESPONSE.—For his mercy, etc.
LEADER.—Who giveth food to all flesh:
RESPONSE.—For his mercy, etc.
LEADER—O give thanks unto the God of heaven:
RESPONSE.—For his mercy, etc.

Flower Song.

E. M. OLLERENSHAW. MELCHIOR TESCHNER, 1615.

1. From mea-dow, and from gar - den We cull the flow'rs of earth,
2. Yet for a ten-d'rer ser - vice These flow-'rets we pre - pare;
3. These earth-ly flow'rs are fad - ing, Yet are they em-blems sweet
And bring them to the foot - stool Of him who gave them birth.
For worn and wea - ry suf - f'rers As to - kens of God's care.
Of ev - er - last - ing flow - ers, For heaven's high service meet;
That by their gen - tle fra - grance, Their col - ors pure and bright,
As mes - sen - gers of com - fort, When faith and hope are dim,
Of love, and hope, and pa - tience, Of faith, and joy - ful praise;
They may show forth the prais - es Of Christ, our Lord and Light.
For he who clothes the li - lies, Bids them still trust in him.
Oh, Sav - iour, make their fragrance ours E'en in our youth - ful days.

Fair as a Lily.

W. L. M. W. L. Mason.

Dolce.

1. All along the hedgerows, nodding in the sun, Come the little flow'rs, one by one;
2. Buttercups and daisies, dandelions too, Smiling in the morning, wet with dew!

In our path we meet them, And their modest grace
Lends joy and charm to ev'ry place.
Oh, the wondrous beauty of these blossoms fair, Which tell us of God's tender care!

CHORUS.

Fair as a lil- y, joyous and free, True as the wild flowers we should be!

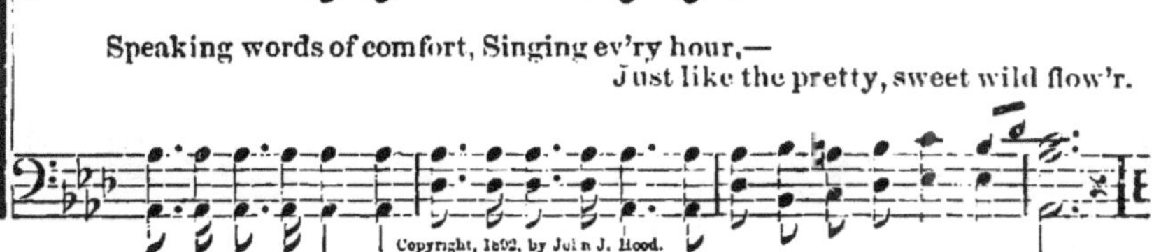
Speaking words of comfort, Singing ev'ry hour,—
Just like the pretty, sweet wild flow'r.
Copyright, 1892, by John J. Hood.

Wont You Love My Jesus?

SALLIE SMITH. JNO. R. SWENEY.

1. I have found a friend di - vine, Wont you love him too?
2. Oh, how dear his name to me, Wont you love him too?
3. Heav - y - la - den, care - oppressed, Wont you love him too?
4. Cast your bur - den at his feet, Wont you love him too?

I am his and he is mine, Wont you love him too?
None can save your soul but he, Wont you love him too?
How he longs to give you rest, Wont you love him too?
There is par - don pure and sweet, Wont you love him too?

CHORUS.

Wont you love my Je - sus, My pre- cious, pre- cious Je - sus?
Wont you love my Je - sus? He is waiting now for you.

Saviour, Blessed Saviour.

GODFREY THWING. HAYDN.

1. Saviour, blessed Saviour, List - en whilst we sing, Hearts and voices
2. Near - er, ev - er near - er, Christ, we draw to thee, Deep in ad - o-
3. Great and ev - er great - er Are thy mercies here; True and ev - er

rais - ing Praises to our King, All we have to of - fer:
ra - tion Bending low the knee: Thou for our re - demp - tion
last - ing Are thy glo - ries there, Where no pain, or sor - row,

All we hope to be, Bod - y, soul, and spir - it, All we
Cam'st on earth to die; Thou, that we might fol - low, Hast gone
Toil or care is known, Where the an - gel le - gions Cir - cle

yield to thee.
up on high.
round thy throne.

CHORUS.

Saviour, bless - ed Sa - viour, List - en, whilst we

sing, Hearts and voi - ces rais - ing Prais - es to our King.

Words of Life.

"The words that I speak unto you, they are spirit, and they are life."
John vi. 63.
W. S. Martin.
J. H. Tenney.
1. Com-ing to cheer us in sad - ness; Coming with bless - ings rife;
2. Loving the message they bring us; Help- ing us on in the way;
3. Blessing on him who shall hear them; Life to the souls who be- lieve;
Com- ing to fill us with glad - ness;—Wonder- ful words of life!
Lead-ing a-long in the dark - ness, Up to the realms of day.
Glo - ry, e - ter - nal, unchang- ing, For all who God's message receive.
CHORUS.
Beau- ti- ful words! wonderful words! Open your hearts to receive them;
Pardon and peace, blessing and grace, Are offered to all who believe them.

Kind Words are Always Best.

"A soft answer turneth away wrath."—Prov. xv: 1.

Eben E. Rexford.
Wm. J. Kirkpatrick.
1. Oh, speak kind words where'er you be, As thro' this world you go, Let
2. Yes, speak kind words in ev - 'ry place, Although you do not know The
3. Then, speak kind words whate'er you do; Too brief is human life To
kind - ly deeds beside your path Like flow'rs of beau - ty grow; The
good your loving words may do To those who need them so; For
waste the hours as they go by In dis - cord and in strife; Give
fragrance of a lov - ing word Will lin - ger in the heart, As
God will know, and sure - ly he In his good time and way, The
one and all a lov - ing word—Just put them to the test, And
sweetness haunts the flow'rs we prize
When summer days depart. Kind words are always best,
giv- er of a helpful word Will royal- ly re- pay.
you will find in ev'ry place Kind words are always best.
CHORUS.
Kind words are always best;
Kind words are always best.
You will find, where'er you go,

Growing up for Jesus.

Priscilla J. Owens. Wm. J. Kirkpatrick.

1. Growing up for Je-sus, we are tru-ly blest, In his smile is welcome, in his arms our rest, In his truth our treasure, in his love to be Growing up for Je-sus in the J. C. E.
2. Not too young to love him, youthful hearts beat true, Not too young to serve him as the dew-drops do, Not too young to praise him, singing as we come, Not too young to answer when he calls us home.
3. Growing up for Je-sus, learning day by day How to fol-low onward in the narrow way; Seeking ho-ly treasure, finding precious truth, Growing up for Je-sus in our hap-py youth.

D.S.—In his truth our treasure, in his love to be Growing up for Je-sus in the J. C. E.
(or this: *in his love our rule, Growing up for Je-sus in our Sunday school.*)

Fine.

CHORUS.

Growing up for Jesus, till in him complete, Growing up for Jesus, oh, his work is sweet:

D.S.

Lift up Your Hearts.

E. A Barnes.
Jno. R. Sweney.
1. Praise the Lord for all his blessings, For the guidance of his hand,
2. Praise him for his ways and do-ings, For the shadow of his wing,
3. Praise him for his love and goodness, For his counsels and his cheer,
4. Praise him for the bless-ed gos-pel, For the way that leads to God,
For his might-y works and wonders That ap-pear on sea and land.
For the seed-time and the har-vest, With the gifts they free-ly bring.
For the hope that shines a-bove us, All a-long our jour-ney here.
For the gift of free sal-va-tion Wrought by his redeem-ing blood.
CHORUS.
Praise the Lord, O ye peo-ple, Walking in his light, Happy in his love,
And with songs that speak his glo-ry, Lift up your hearts to God.

Onward and Upward.

E. E. Hewitt.
Jno. R. Sweney.
1. Onward still, and upward, Follow ev - ermore Where our mighty Leader Goes in love before; "Looking unto Je - sus," Reach a helping hand To a struggling neighbor, Helping him to stand.
2. Onward, ev - er onward, Thro' the pastures green, Where the streams flow softly, Under skies serene; Or, if need be, upward, O'er the rocky steep, Trusting him who guides us, Strong to save and keep.
3. Upward, ev - er upward, T'ward the radiant glow, Far a - bove the valley, Where the mist hangs low; On, with songs of gladness, Till the march shall end, Where ten thousand thousand Hallelu - jahs blend.
CHORUS.
Marching on - - ward, up - - ward, Marching steadi - ly, onward, Je - sus leads the way, Marching on - ward,
Marching on- ward, marching onward, on - ward, Up - ward march- ing, up - ward, up- ward,
onward, march- ing on-ward, on- ward,

up - - ward, Onward unto glory, To the perfect day.
upward, marching upward, upward,
Little Friends of Jesus.
S. Martin.
Wm. J. Kirkpatrick.
1. Do you know what makes us hap-py, When so man - y hearts are sad?
2. Je - sus loves the children dear - ly,— In his Word he tells them so;
3. We are lit - tle lambs of Je - sus: He, our Shepherd kind and dear,
4. If we try our best to please him He will take us by and by
We are lit - tle friends of Je - sus, That is why we are so glad.
Once he took them up and blessed them, Many, man - y years a - go.
Speaks, and, though we do not see him, In our hearts his voice we hear.
Where our spir - it eyes will know him, Far beyond the star - ry sky.
CHORUS.
We are lit- tle friends, we are loving friends, We are happy, hap- py lit - tle
friends of Jesus; We are little friends, we are loving friends, We are happy all day long.

Winning Precious Souls.

Elizabeth Stillwell. Adam Geibel.

1. Winning precious souls for Je - sus, Blessed priv- i- lege and joy!
2. Winning precious souls for Je - sus, Let us la- bor at his side;
3. Winning precious souls for Je - sus, Cul- ti- vate the gospel art;
Sharing in the Master's mis - sion, Let us ev- 'ry power em- ploy.
He will make his people fruit - ful, When they in his love a - bide.
Us- ing ev- 'ry right en - deav - or, With a patient, lov - ing heart;
Seeking, in our conscious weakness, Strength and guidance, day by day,
Let us follow as he leads us, Read- y for the moment's call,
Be it ours to bring the Mas - ter Jewels that will shine on high,
CHORUS.
He will give the needed wisdom, Teach us what to do and say. Winning precious
By the wayside, as we journey, Let the seeds of blessing fall.
Stars to sparkle for his glory, When he crowns us, by and by.
Winning precious souls, [winning
souls, winning precious souls for Jesus, Winning precious souls, winning precious souls [for
precious souls,
Winning precious souls, winning precious souls,

Winning Precious Souls.—CONCLUDED. 151
Jesus,—Stars to sparkle for his glo - ry, Jewels that will shine on high;
Stars to sparkle for his glory, When he crowns us in his kingdom, by and by.
Call us Thine own.
Fanny J Crosby.
Wm. J. Kirkpatrick.
1. Dear Saviour, we gath - er Once more at thy throne; Oh, hear us, we pray thee, Now make us thine own.
2. Dear Saviour, thy promise We tru - ly be - lieve: Who- ev - er will seek thee Shall mercy re - ceive.
3. Dear Saviour, behold us, In thee would we hide; We ask that thy Spir - it In us may a - bide.
4. Dear Saviour, we love thee, Thy name we a - dore; Oh, grant us thy bless - ing, Thy joy ev - er - more.
CHORUS.
Here grateful- ly bend- ing, Sweet mel- o- dy blending, Come, oh, come, tender - ly Call us thine own.

O Sing Unto the Lord.

E. E. Hewitt. Jno. R. Sweney.

SEMI-CHORUS.
O sing un- to the Lord a new song:
CHORUS.
Sing un- to the Lord, all the earth.
SEMI-CHORUS.
Sing un- to the Lord,
CHORUS.
bless his ho - ly name; Show forth his sal- va- tion from day to day.
SEMI-CHORUS.
De- clare his glo - ry a - mong the heath - en,
CHORUS.
His won -

SEMI-CHORUS.
ders a-mong all peo-ple: De-clare his glo-ry a-
CHORUS.
mong the heath-en, His won-ders a-mong all peo-ple.
Bring Them In.
ALEXCENAH THOMAS.
W. A. OGDEN.
1. Hark! 'tis the Shepherd's voice I hear, Out in the desert dark and drear,
2. Who'll go and help this Shepherd kind, Help him the wand'ring lambs to find?
2. Out in the desert hear their cry; Out on the mountain wild and high,
Calling the lambs who've gone astray, Far from the Shepherd's fold away.
Who'll bring the lost ones to the fold, Where they'll be sheltered from the cold?
Hark! 'tis the Master speaks to thee, "Go, find my lambs, where'er they be."
CHORUS.
1st.
2d.
Bring them in, bring them in, Bring them in from the fields of sin;
Bring them in, bring them in, Bring the wand'ring ones to . . Jesus.

From "Notes of Victory," by per. of W. A. Ogden.

Good By.

E. E. Hewitt. Wm. J. Kirkpatrick.

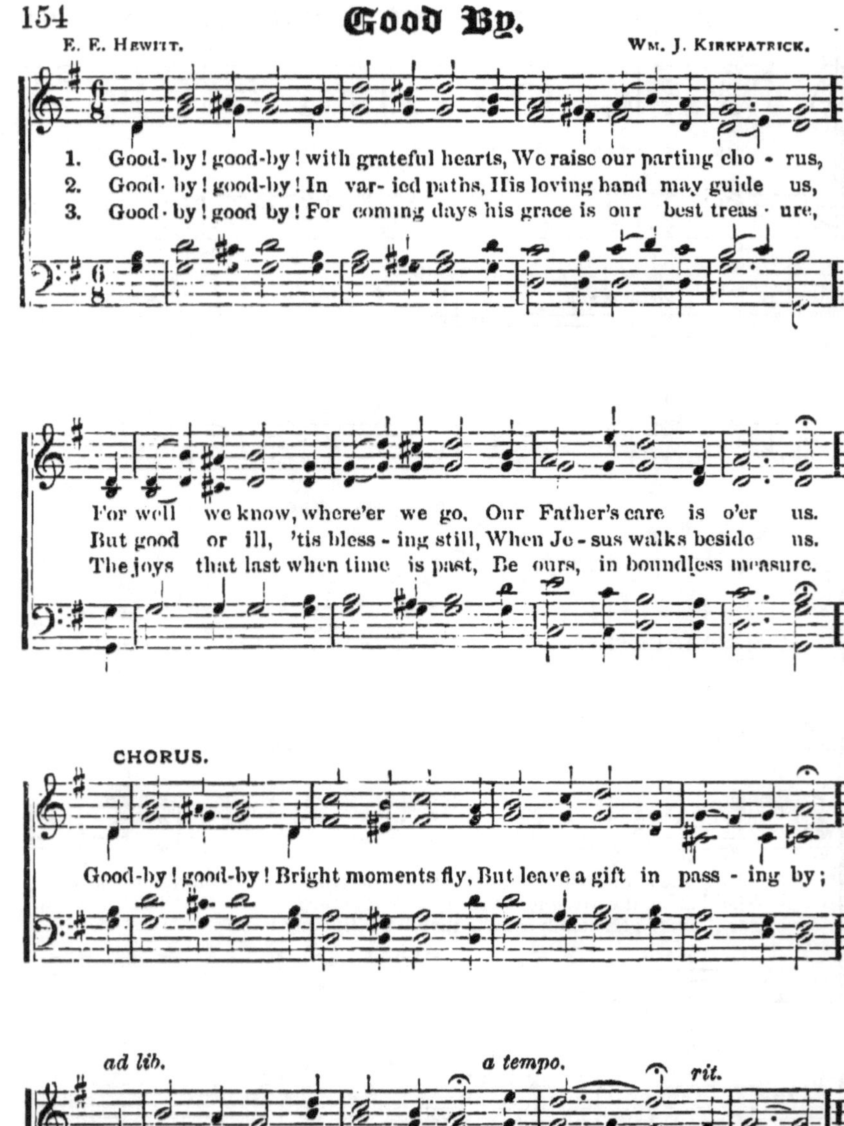
1. Good-by! good-by! with grateful hearts, We raise our parting cho - rus,
2. Good-by! good-by! In var-ied paths, His loving hand may guide us,
3. Good-by! good by! For coming days his grace is our best treas - ure,
For well we know, where'er we go, Our Father's care is o'er us.
But good or ill, 'tis bless - ing still, When Je - sus walks beside us.
The joys that last when time is past, Be ours, in boundless measure.
CHORUS.
Good-by! good-by! Bright moments fly, But leave a gift in pass - ing by;
ad lib.
a tempo.
rit.
God bless us all, God bless us all, Good-by, ... good - by.
good by

God be with You.

"The grace of our Lord Jesus Christ be with you." Rom. xvi. 20.

J. E. Rankin, D. D. — W. G. Tomer.

1. God be with you till we meet again, By his counsels guide, uphold you,
2. God be with you till we meet again, 'Neath his wings securely hide you;
3. God be with you till we meet again, When life's perils thick confound you;
4. God be with you till we meet again, Keep love's banner floating o'er you;
With his sheep securely fold you, God be with you till we meet again.
Dai - ly manna still provide you, God be with you till we meet again.
Put his arms unfailing round you, God be with you till we meet again.
Smite death's threat'ning wave before you, God be with you till we meet again.
CHORUS.
Till we meet, till we meet, Till we meet at Je - sus' feet;
Till we meet, till we meet, till we meet, till we meet;
Till we meet, till we meet, God be with you till we meet again.
Till we meet, till we meet, till we meet,

From "Gospel Bells," by per.

Praise God.

Jno. R. Sweney.

Praise God, from whom all blessings flow, Praise the Lord, praise the Lord!
Praise, him all creatures here be- low, Praise the Lord, praise the Lord;
rit.
Praise him above, ye heavenly host; Praise Father, Son, and Ho- ly Ghost;
Praise Fa - ther, Son, and Ho - ly Ghost. Halle - lu - jah! halle-
Praise Father, Son and Ho - ly Ghost. Hallelujah!
lu - jah! hal - le- lu - jah! a - men; Hal - le - lu - jah! hal - le-
hal- le- lu- jah! hal- le- lu- jah! Hal- le- lu- jah!

rit.
lu - jah! halle- lujah! amen; Amen, amen, Halle- lu- jah! a- men.
hallelujah!
Hallelujah!
Come, let us Sing.
L. H. EDMUNDS.
JNO. R. SWENEY.
1. Come, let us sing re- deeming love, Blessed be the name of the Lord;
2. He hid me in the liv- ing Rock, Blessed be the name of the Lord;
3. He put this song with- in my soul, Blessed be the name of the Lord;
Sing with the raptured hosts a- bove, Blessed be the name of the Lord.
And leads me with his hap- py flock, Blessed be the name of the Lord.
Let heavenly hal - le - lujahs roll, Blessed be the name of the Lord.
CHORUS.
Lift up the heart, lift up the voice, Praise ye the Lord, rejoice, rejoice!
Come, let us sing in sweet ac - cord, Blessed be the name of the Lord.

Another Song for Jesus.

E. E. Hewitt. — Wm. J. Kirkpatrick.

1. An- oth - er song for Je - sus, A hymn of faith and love, To
2. O let us ev - er lin - ger Beside joy's radiant spring, So
3. An- oth - er song for Je - sus, A song of love and praise, And

wing our grateful prais- es To glo- ry-realms above. We thank thee, precious
pure, so fresh, 'tis flowing For all who love our King. How sweet are fleeting
let the blessed mu - sic Re- echo thro' life's days. We'll sing his tender

Saviour, For hap- py hours like this, For Elim-bowers of gladness, And
pleasures, When hallowed by his smile! How rich e- ter- nal treasures, Be-
mercies, Un- til our voices blend With those of saints and angels, Where

heaven's exceeding bliss.
yond time's "little while."
praises have no end.

CHORUS.

Anoth - er song for Je - sus, A hymn of faith and love, To wing our grateful prais - es To glo- ry-realms a - bove.

Friends, Good-night!

E. E. Hewitt.
Jno. R. Sweney.
1. Friends, good-night! friends, good-night! Swiftly these hours of reunion fly;
2. Precious hours, precious hours, Flinging their light o'er our passing days;
3. Friends, good-night! friends, good-night! When shadows darken we'll look above;
Cho.–Friends, good-night! friends, good-night! Blessed reunions, too soon they fly.
Fine.
Friends, good-night! friends, good-night! Lift we our pray'r on high.
Precious hours, precious hours, Close them with pray'r and praise.
Friends, good-night! Friends, good-night! Safe in his arms of love.
Friends, good-night! friends, good-night! Je- sus is ev - er nigh.
May our Father bless you, Mercy and peace Richly increase,
May our Father bless you, Jesus has bought Treasures unthought,
May our Father bless you, Happy farewell, Happy farewell,
D. C. Chorus.
God our Fa - ther bless you, Bless you ev - er - more.
Copyright, 1890, by Jno. R. Sweney.

160
Just as I am.
M. Farningham.
Dedicated to Mr. Wm. S. Ferguson.
Jno. R. Sweney.
1. "Just as I am," thine own to be, Friend of the young, who lovest me:
2. In the glad morning of my day, My life to give, my vows to pay,
3. I would live ev - er in the light, I would work ever for the right,
4. "Just as I am," young, strong and free, To be the best that I can be
To con - se - crate myself to thee, O Je - sus Christ, I come, I come.
With no re - serve and no de - lay, With all my heart I come, I come.
I would serve thee with all my might, Therefore to thee I come, I come.
For truth, and righteousness, and thee, Lord of my life, I come, I come.
CHORUS.
Repeat pp.
Just as I am, . . . Just as I am. . . . Just as I am, . . . O Lord, I come.
Just as I am,
Just as I am,
Just as I am,
161
The Lord is my Shepherd.
A - men.

1 The Lord is my Shepherd ; I | shall not | want. || He maketh me to lie down in green pastures : He leadeth me beside the still | wa- | ters.

2 He restoreth my soul : He leadeth me in the paths of righteousness for his | name's | sake. || Yea, though I walk through the valley of the shadow of death, I will fear no evil : for thou art with me ; Thy rod and thy staff they | comfort | me.

3 Thou preparest a table before me in the presence of mine enemies : Thou anointest my head with oil ; my | cup runneth | over. || Surely goodness and mercy shall follow me all the days of my life : And I will dwell in the house of the Lord for- | ev- | er. || A- | men.

162 P. DODDRIDGE. Happy Day. English Melody.

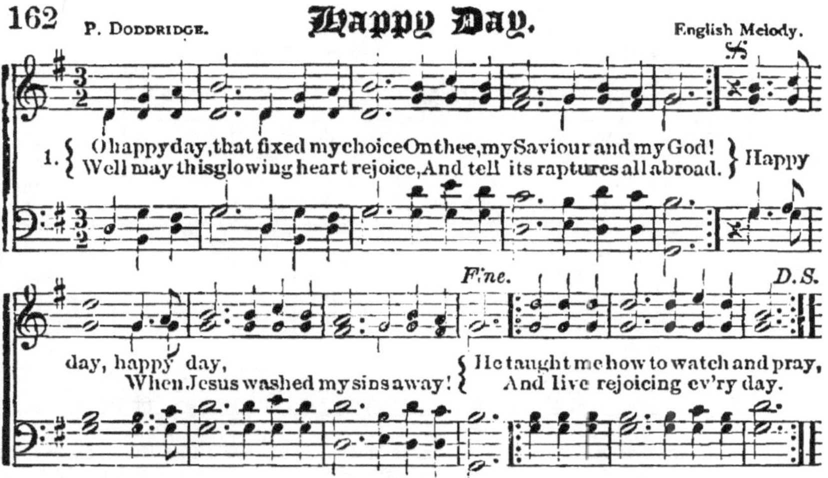
1. { O happy day, that fixed my choice On thee, my Saviour and my God!
Well may this glowing heart rejoice, And tell its raptures all abroad. } Happy
day, happy day,
When Jesus washed my sins away! { He taught me how to watch and pray,
And live rejoicing ev'ry day.
Fine.
D.S.

2 O happy bond, that seals my vows
To him who merits all my love!
Let cheerful anthems fill his house,
While to that sacred shrine I move.

3 'Tis done! the great transaction's done!
I am my Lord's, and he is mine:
He drew me, and I followed on,
Charmed to confess that voice divine.

4 Now rest, my long-divided heart;
Fixed on this blissful center, rest;
Nor ever from thy Lord depart;
With him of every good possessed.

5 High heav'n that heard the solemn vow,
That vow renewed shall daily hear,
Till in life's latest hour I bow,
And bless in death a bond so dear.

163 H. E. BLAIR He Came to Save Me. WM. J. KIRKPATRICK.

1st.
2d.
1. { When Jesus laid his crown aside, He came to save me;
When on the cross he bled and died, ... He came to save me.
2. { In my poor heart he deigns to dwell, He came to save me;
Oh, praise his name, I know it well, ... He came to save me.
REFRAIN.
1st.
2d.
I'm so glad, I'm so glad, I'm so glad that Jesus came, And grace is free,
He . . . came to save me.

3 With gentle hand he leads me still,
He came to save me;
And trusting him I fear no ill,
He came to save me.

4 To him my faith with rapture clings,
He came to save me;
To him my heart looks up and sings,
He came to save me.

Junior Songs—L

164
The Golden Key.
"Prayer is the key to unlock the door, and the bolt to shut in the night."
Jno. R. Sweney.
1. Prayer is the key For the bending knee To open the morn's first hours;
2. Not a soul so sad, Nor a heart so glad, When cometh the shades of night,
3. Take the golden key In your hand and see, As the night tide drifts away,
See the incense rise To the starry skies, Like per-fume from the flow'rs.
But the daybreak song Will the joy prolong, And some darkness turn to light.
How its blessed hold Is a crown of gold, Thro' the weary hours of day.
4 When the shadows fall,
And the vesper call
Is sobbing its low refrain,
'Tis a garland sweet
To the toil dent feet,
And an antidote for pain
5 Soon the year's dark door
Shall be shut no more:
Life's tears shall be wiped away,
As the pearl gates swing,
And the gold harps ring,
And the sun unsheathe for aye.
Copyright, 1876, by John J. Hood.
165 T. O'N
Song to the Trinity.
Thos. O'Neill.
1. Fa-ther, hear us in our song of praise, Help us join with heart and voice;
2. Blessed Je-sus, to thy children come, While we praise thy glorious name;
3. Thou, by whom we reach the Father's ear, Thro' the Saviour's loving heart;
Grate-ful melo-dy to thee we raise, In heaven-ly harmon-y re-joice.
Make our youthful, tender hearts thy home, And there, dear Saviour, ever reign.
In whate'er is to thy children dear, Thou, Spir-it, hast a vi-tal part.
Copyright, 1888, by John J. Hood.

Song to the Trinity.—CONCLUDED.
CHORUS.
Hal - le - lu - jah! praise the Fa - ther; Hal-le - lu - jah! praise the Son;
rit.
And thou, Ho - ly Spir - it, We praise thee; Three in One. A - men.
166
There is a Glorious World.
JANE TAYLOR.
J. H. KURZENKNABE.
1. There is a glo-rious world of light, A - bove the star - ry sky,
2. Those are the hymns that we shall know, If Je - sus we o - bey!
3. This is the joy we ought to seek, And make our chief concern;
4. Great God, impress us ev - 'ry day, That nothing may al - lure;
Fine.
Where saints de - part - ed, clothed in white, A - dore the Lord most High.
That is the place where we shall go, If found in wisdom's way.
For this we come, from week to week, To read, and hear, and learn.
But both the taught and teachers may Make their sal - va - tion sure.
D.S.—Ten thousand, thousand chil - dren join, And all is per - fect praise.
CHORUS.
D.S.
And hark! a - mid the sa - cred songs Those heavenly voic - es raise,

167 I'll Live for Him.

C. R. DUNBAR.

1. My life, my love I give to thee, Thou Lamb of God, who died for me;
2. I now believe thou dost receive, For thou hast died that I might live;
3. Oh, thou who died on Cal - va - ry, To save my soul and make me free,

CHO.—I'll live for him who died for me, How happy then my life shall be!

D.C.
Oh, may I ev - er faith - ful be, My Sav - iour and my God!
And now henceforth I'll trust in thee, My Sav - iour and my God!
I con - se - crate my life to thee, My Sav - iour and my God!

I'll live for him who died for me, My Sav iour and my God!

168 Happy Land.

OLD MELODY.

1. { There is a hap - py land, Far, far a - way.
Where saints in glory stand, Bright, bright as day; }
Oh, how they sweetly sing,
"Worthy is our Saviour King," Loud let his praises ring, Praise, praise for aye!

2 Bright, in that happy land,
Beams every eye;
Kept by a Father's hand,
Love cannot die.
On, then, to glory run;
Be a crown and kingdom won;
And bright, above the sun,
Reign evermore.

3 Come to that happy land,
Come, come away;
Why will you doubting stand?
Why still delay?
Oh, we shall happy be,
When from sin and sorrow free;
Lord, we shall dwell with thee,
Blest evermore.

169 We will Follow On.

E. R. Latta. Wm. J. Kirkpatrick.

1. Where the Saviour's hand is leading, We will fol- low, fol- low on;
His commands and warnings heeding, We will follow on.

2. Where the Saviour's voice is calling, We will fol- low, fol- low on;
Show'rs of grace upon us falling, We will follow on.

3. In the way the star is showing, We will fol- low, fol- low on;
To celestial mansions going, We will follow on.

4. Still by faith our way pur- su- ing, We will fol- low, fol- low on;
Glad the land of promise viewing, We will follow on.

5. 'Neath the cross to - geth- er banding, We will fol- low, fol- low on;
Ever toward the golden landing, We will follow on.

CHORUS.

Follow on, follow on,
Till the heav'nly prize is won; Till we grasp a shining crown, Follow, follow on.

170 Psalm CXIX: 1-6. C. M.

Tune No. 166.

How blest are they whose lives are pure,
And upright in the way,
Who in the Lord's most holy law
Do walk and do not stray.

2 O blest are they who to observe
His statues are inclined;
And who do seek the living God,
With their whole heart and mind.

3 Such in his ways do walk, and they
Do no iniquity.
Thou hast commanded us to keep
Thy precepts carefully.

4 O that thy statutes to observe
Thou wouldst my way direct!
Then shall I not be 'shamed, when I
Thy precepts all respect.

5 Then with integrity of heart
Thee will I praise and bless,
When I the judgments all have learned
Of thy pure righteousness.

6 That I will keep thy statutes all,
Firmly resolved have I:
O do not then, most gracious God,
Forsake me utterly.

171 Lead Me, Precious Saviour.

Mrs. J. F. K. | Mrs. Jos. F. Knapp. By per.

1. Lead me, lead me, Lead me, precious Saviour, In- to the narrow way, In-
2. I will love thee, Ev- er, ev- er love thee; May sinful thoughts depart, Oh,
3. Lead me, fold me, Guide, and ever keep me, And thanks my heart will give, Dear
CHORUS.
to the narrow way, Fold me, fold me, Fold me to thy bo - som, And
take them from my heart.
Saviour, while I live.
may I never stray, oh, nev - er stray, And I will praise thee ev- ermore, yes,
ev - er - more, And I will praise thee ev- ermore, yes, ev - er - more.

172 Psalm CXLV. L. M. *Tune "Migdol."*

The Lord our God most gracious is,
  In him compassions also flow;
In mercy he is rich to bless,
  But unto anger he is slow.

2 To all the Lord is very good,
  O'er all his works his mercy is.
Thy works all praise to thee afford: [bless
  Thy saints, O Lord, thy name shall

3 Thy kingdom's glory they shall show,
  They also shall thy power tell.
That so men's sons his deeds may know,
  His kingdom's grace that doth excel.

4 Thy kingdom hath no end at all,
  It shall to ages all remain.
The Lord upholdeth all that fall,
  The cast-down raiseth up again.

173 O Receive Him.

Lizzie Edwards. Jno. R. Sweney.

1. Youthful voic- es, happy voic - es, Sing of Je - sus and his love,
2. Youthful voic- es, happy voic - es, While we praise him day by day,
3. Youthful voic- es, happy voic - es, While we breathe his name so dear,

Fine.

While the an - gels bending o'er us Whisper soft - ly from a - bove,—
Lo! the an - gels hov - er round us; In our hearts we hear them say,—
From the Bi - ble, ho - ly Bi - ble, Still the gen - tle words we hear,—

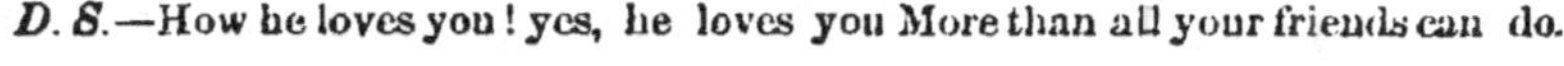
D. S.—How he loves you! yes, he loves you More than all your friends can do.

Chorus.

D. S.
Oh, believe him, oh, receive him, Your Redeem - er kind and true!

174 Psalm CXII. *Tune "Beulah Land."*

How blest the man that fears the Lord,
And makes his law his chief delight;
His seed shall share his great reward,
And on the earth be men of might.

Cho.—How blest the man that fears the Lord,
And makes his law his chief delight;
‖: His seed shall share his great reward,
And on the earth be men of might. :‖

2 Abounding wealth shall bless his home,
His righteousness shall still endure;
To him shall light arise in gloom;
He's kind, compassionate and pure.

3 The good will favor show, and lend,
And his affairs discreetly guide:
Unmoved he stands till life shall end,
His name and honor shall abide.

4 No evil tidings shall he fear;
His heart doth on the Lord repose;
He stands unmoved by dangers near,
Till he shall see his prostrate foes.

5 Dispersing gifts among the poor,
His lib'ral hands their wants supply;
His righteousness shall still endure,
His pow'r shall be exalted high.

6 The wicked shall his honor see,
Consume with grief, and gnash and wail;
Their hopes shall disappointed be,
And their desires forever fail.

175 Loving Jesus.
H. L. B.
Harry L. Brooks.
1. I love to sing of Je - sus, Because he died for me; It grieves my heart to think that he Should die up - on a tree.
2. I love to sing of Je - sus, For tho' he's gone above, He lis- tens to my fee- ble praise, And shields me with his love.
3. And if on earth we're faithful, In heaven his face we'll see, And sing, in songs more joy - ful, Through all e - ter- ni - ty.
Oh, lov - ing Je - sus! Je - sus! Je - sus! Oh, lov - ing Je - sus! I'll on - ly sing of thee.
176 Num. vi. 24-26. The Lord Bless Thee. W. J. K.
A blessing for use in closing Sabbath-school, or other service, in the absence of a minister.
The Lord bless thee, and keep thee: The Lord make his face shine upon thee and be [gracious unto thee: The Lord lift up his countenance upon thee, and give thee peace. Amen.

177 Onward March.

"Fight the good fight of faith."—1 Tim. vi. 12.

Mrs. R. N. Turner. Wm. J. Kirkpatrick.

1. In the bat-tle-field of life, Junior, take thy place; When thy foes be-fore thee rise Meet them face to face.
2. Raise thy banner high and free, Christ shall lead thee on, Safe thro' all the storm of war, Till the vict'ry's won.
3. Clad in ar-mor of the Lord, Read-y for the foe, Shield and breast-plate strong and sure, Onward, Christian, go!
CHORUS.
Onward march! onward march! Cross of Christ thy sign; Forward march! forward march! Vict'ry shall be thine!

4 See, thine enemies approach,
Armies of the world!
Meet them bravely, meet them well,
With thy flag unfurled!

5 Onward, Christian, for the war,
Join the noble fight;
Christ shall lead the army forth,—
Battle for the right!

178 Psalm XI. S. M. *Tune "Ferguson."*

My trust is in the Lord;
How to my soul say ye,
Away with speed, and like a bird
To your high mountain flee?

2 Lo, sinners bend the bow;
On string they fit the dart,
That they unseen may shoot at those
Who upright are in heart.

3 What can the righteous do?
What can for them avail,
If the foundations be destroyed
And all they built on fail?

4 The Lord in Zion dwells,
The Lord's throne is on high:
His eyes behold the sons of men;
Yea, them his eyelids try.

179 Shout Hosanna!
J. J. L.
J. J. Lowe.
1. Children once were heard to sing Welcome un - to Israel's King,
2. Oh, how glad - ly we should try, When the Lord is passing by,
3. Je - sus, thou art still the same, Still thou dost thy love proclaim;
When so man - y si - lent were, Their ho - san - nas fill'd the air.
Some kind sign of love to bring, And ho - san - nas loud - ly sing.
Oh, come vis - it us to - day, En - ter ev - 'ry heart we pray.
CHORUS.
Shout ho- sanna un- to David's Son! Shout ho- sanna as with joy we sing!
Shout hosanna! shout hosanna! Shout ho- sanna unto Christ our King!
Copyright, 1892, by J. J. Lowe.
180 Blessed Jesus.
Anon.
Wm. J. Kirkpatrick.
1. Blessed Je - sus, meek and mild, Stoop to hear a lit - tle child;
2. Take a - way my load of sin, Make me clean and pure within;
3. In my childhood may I be Gen - tle, meek and pure like thee;
4. Ten- der- Je - sus, thou didst call To thine arms the children small;
Copyright, 1892, by Wm. J. Kirkpatrick.

Blessed Jesus.—CONCLUDED.

At thy feet I come to pray, Saviour, cast me not a - way.
Teach me all I need to know, Be my Shepherd here be - low.
Help me ev - 'ry sin to leave, Lest thy lov- ing heart I grieve.
Lo, I come, and humbly pray, Saviour, cast me not a - way.
181
All for Jesus.
Mary D. James.
Jno. R. Sweney.
1. All for Je - sus! all for Je - sus! All my being's ransomed powers:
2. Let my hands perform his bidding, Let my feet run in his ways—
2. Worldlings prize their gems of beauty, Cling to gild- ed toys of dust,
4. Since my eyes were fixed on Je - sus, I've lost sight of all be- sides;
5. Oh, what wonder! how a - mazing! Je - sus, glorious King of kings—
Fine.
All my thoughts, and words, and doings, All my days, and all my hours.
Let my eyes see Je - sus on - ly, Let my lips speak forth his praise.
Boast of wealth, and fame, and pleasure: On - ly Je - sus will I trust.
So enchained my spirit's vis- ion, Looking at the Cru- ci - fied.
Deigns to call me his be- lov - ed, Lets me rest beneath his wings.
D.S.—All for Je - sus! blessed Je - sus! I am his, and he is mine.
CHORUS.
D.S.
All for Je - sus! blessed Je - sus! All for Je - sus, gladly I resign;

182 Thankful Hearts.
May F. Williams.
Jno. R. Sweney.
1. Thankful hearts to-day we bring, Dear, loving Saviour; Help us now thy praise to sing, Dear, loving Saviour.
2. In thy tender, watchful care, Dear, loving Saviour; Fold and keep us safely there, Dear, loving Saviour.
3. Nev - er let a naughty word, Dear, loving Saviour; From our youthful lips be heard, Dear, loving Saviour.
4. Train us up to live with thee, Dear, loving Saviour; Where thy glory we shall see, Dear, loving Saviour.
CHORUS.
Keep thy children now, we pray, Ever in the shining way, Lead us gen- tly ev- 'ry day, Dear, loving Saviour.
Copyright, 1892, by Jno. R. Sweney.
183 I am the Resurrection.
I am the resur- rection . . . and the life; He that believeth in me, tho' he were . . dead, yet shall he live; and whosoever liveth and . . believeth in me, shall nev - er die.

187 The Morning Light.

Samuel F. Smith. Tune, WEBB. 7. 6.

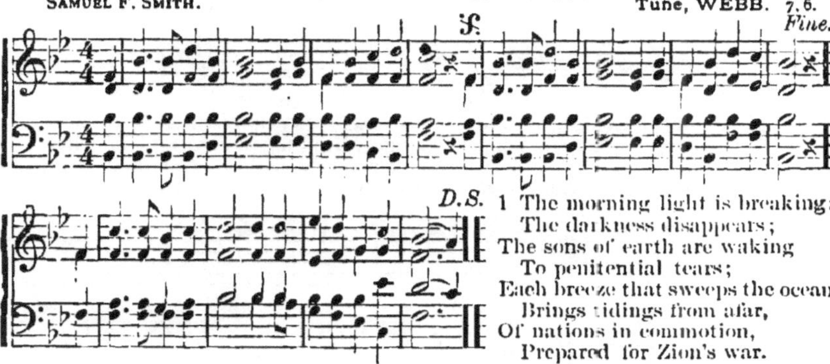

1 The morning light is breaking:
The darkness disappears;
The sons of earth are waking
To penitential tears;
Each breeze that sweeps the ocean
Brings tidings from afar,
Of nations in commotion,
Prepared for Zion's war.

2 See heathen nations bending
Before the God we love,
And thousand hearts ascending
In gratitude above;
While sinners, now confessing,
The gospel call obey,
And seek the Saviour's blessing,
A nation in a day.

3 Blest river of salvation,
Pursue thine onward way;
Flow thou to every nation,
Nor in thy richness stay:
Stay not till all the lowly
Triumphant reach their home:
Stay not till all the holy
Proclaim, "The Lord is come!"

188 Stand up, stand up for Jesus.

Geo. Duffield, Jr. Tune above.

1 Stand up, stand up for Jesus,
Ye soldiers of the cross;
Lift high his royal banner,
It must not suffer loss;
From victory unto victory
His army shall he lead
Till every foe is vanquished
And Christ is Lord indeed.

2 Stand up, stand up for Jesus,
The trumpet call obey;
Forth to the mighty conflict,
In this his glorious day:
"Ye that are men, now serve him,"
Against unnumbered foes:
Your courage rise with danger,
And strength to strength oppose.

3 Stand up, stand up for Jesus,
Stand in his strength alone;
The arm of flesh will fail you;
Ye dare not trust your own:
Put on the gospel armor,
Each piece put on with prayer;
Where duty calls, or danger,
Be never wanting there.

4 Stand up, stand up for Jesus,
The strife will not be long;
This day the noise of battle,
The next the victor's song:
To him that overcometh,
A crown of life shall be;
He with the King of glory
Shall reign eternally.

189 When, His Salvation Bringing.

1 When, his salvation bringing,
To Zion Jesus came,
The children all stood singing
Hosannas to his name.
Nor did their zeal offend him,
For as he rode along,
He let them still attend him,
And smiled to hear their song.

2 And since the Lord retaineth
His love for children still;
Though now as King he reigneth
On Zion's heavenly hill,
We'll flock around his banner,
Who sits upon the throne;
And cry aloud "Hosanna
To David's royal Son!"

3 For should we fail proclaiming
Our great Redeemer's praise:
The stones, our silence shaming
Might well hosannas raise.
But shall we only render
The tribute of our words?
No! while our hearts are tender,
They, too, shall be the Lord's.

190 Tender Saviour.

E. E. Hewitt. Wm. J. Kirkpatrick.

1. Tender Saviour, by whose childhood Ev - 'ry boy and girl is blest,
2. Hold us by thy hand, dear Saviour, Lead us in thy ho - ly ways;
3. Walking in thy gen - tle footsteps, Help us, Lord, to follow thee;
4. Make our youth time bright with sunshine, Keep us by thy favor blest,

Help us love and trust and serve thee, Fold us to thy gen - tle breast.
Growing in thy grace and wisdom, Fill our hearts with joyful praise.
Make us pure and true and lov - ing, Make us more and more like thee.
And when earthly life is o - ver Fold us to thy gen - tle breast.

Ten - der Saviour, lov - ing Saviour, Fold us to thy gen - tle breast.
Ten - der Saviour, lov - ing Saviour, Fill our hearts with joyful praise.
Ten - der Saviour, lov - ing Saviour, Make us more and more like thee.
Ten - der Saviour, lov - ing Saviour, Fold us to thy gen - tle breast.

191 Children of Zion.

Mrs. E. C. Ellsworth. Chas. Edw. Prior.

DUET. *Cheerfully.*

1. Oh, many, many children In Zion shall be found; We hear their happy
2. Oh, who will be the children Within the city bright? Will you be one to
3. Then come and bring a playmate, Perchance a brother dear; Let sisters come to-

voi - ces, And pleasant is the sound; For children can be Christians, And
en - ter, And come by morning light? Oh, do not wait till old - er— The
geth - er. Oh, nev - er, nev - er fear; For Zi - on must have children Up-

Children of Zion.—CONCLUDED.
while at work, or play, Be gen- tle like the Master, And all his words obey.
shadows may appear —You may not see to en- ter When night is almost here.
on her golden street, Then come, and bring in with you Whoever you may meet
CHORUS.
Oh, children, come to Jesus! His service is a joy;
Oh, come within the city, Yes, ev'ry girl and boy.
192
For Jesus.
C. H. G.
CHAS. H. GABRIEL.
1. We want to live for Je- sus, A life of ser-vice true, And try to show his
2. We want to work for Je- sus, Because he loved us so; We want to do his
3. We want to die in Je- sus, When all our work is o'er, And go to live for-
CHORUS.
glo- ry In ev-ery thing we do.
pleasure, In all our life below.
ever, On heaven's shining shore.
We want to live work die for Jesus, His children
we would be; We love to sing his praises, For his loy- al ones are we.

193 Jesus Calls Us.

Mary D. James. Jno R. Sweney. By per.

1. Je - sus calls us, list - en, list- en, See the loving Saviour's charms;
2. Je - sus loves us—how he's longing Now to fold us to his breast,
3. He will take us to those mansions, Beauti- ful, prepared on high;
Let the children come, he's say - ing, Now we'll hasten to his arms.
Let us go to our dear Saviour, In his arms we'll sweetly rest.
There we'll live with him for - ev - er, Far a- bove the a - zure sky.
CHORUS.
O, come, let us go, let us go, let us go, Hark! how he's calling us. Hark! how he's
calling us, Come, let us go, let us go, let us go, Come, let us go to Je - sus.

194

Psalm CIII, 8s, 7s. *Tune, "What a Friend we have."*

Far as east from west is distant
He hath put away our sin;
Like the pity of a Father
Hath the Lord's compassion been.
Well he knows our frame, rememb'ring
We are dust, our days like grass;
Man is like the flower blooming,
Till the hot winds o'er it pass.

2 Then 'tis gone, and is remembered
By its former place no more;
But on them that fear Jehovah
Rests his mercy evermore.
As it was without beginning,
So it lasts without an end;
To their children's children ever,
Shall his righteousness extend.

3 Unto such as keep his cov'nant,
And are steadfast in his way;
Unto those who still remember
His commandments and obey.
In the heavens high, Jehovah
Hath for him prepared a throne,
And throughout his vast dominion
All his works his power shall own.

195 Yield not to Temptation.

H. R. PALMER. By per.

1. Yield not to tempta - tion, For yielding is sin, Each vict'ry will help you some oth- er to win; Fight manfully onward, Dark passions sub- due, Look ev- er to Je- sus, He'll car-ry you through.
2. Shun e - vil companions, Bad language disdain, God's name hold in rev'rence, nor take it in vain; Be thoughtful and earnest, Kind-hearted and true,
3. To him that o'ercometh God giveth a crown, Thro' faith we will conquer, though often cast down; He who is our Saviour, Our strength will renew,
CHORUS.
Ask the Saviour to help you, Comfort, strengthen, and keep you, He is willing to aid you, He will carry you through.

196 Psalm XX. C. M.

Tune "Only Trust Him."

JEHOVAH hear thee in the day
When trouble he doth send;
And let the name of Jacob's God
From every ill defend.

2 In thy salvation we will joy,
In our God's name we will
Display our banners; and the Lord
Thy prayers all fulfil.

3 O let him send his help to thee
Out from his holy place;
Let him from Zion, his own hill,
Sustain thee by his grace.

4 Let him remember all thy gifts,
Accept thy sacrifice;
Grant thee thy heart's wish, and fulfil
Thy thoughts and counsel wise

5 Now know I God his king doth save;
He from his holy heav'n
Will hear him, with the saving strength
By his own right hand giv'n.

6 In chariots some put confidence,
On horses some rely,
But we remember will the name
Of God, our God Most High.

Father all Holy.

E. E. Hewitt. THE LORD'S PRAYER. Wm. J. Kirkpatrick.

1. Father all ho - ly, bend we so lowly, Glowing with love's tender flame,
2. Angels adore thee, waiting before thee, Swift thy commands to fulfil:
3. From sin deliv - er, keep us forev - er, Kingdom and glory are thine,

Father in heaven, praises be giv - en, Hallowed forev - er thy Name.
Grant us, we pray thee, grace to obey thee, Choosing and serving thy will.
Thine, too, the power, hear us this hour, Father, our Father divine!

Telling the story, spreading thy glory, Send forth thy people, we pray,
Father, now lead us, day by day feed us, Ever provide and defend;
Jesus is pleading, still interceding For his redeemed ones again,

Till every nation know thy salvation, Under thy kingdom's full sway.
Trespass confessing, seeking thy blessing, Pardon and peace without end.
For his sake hear us, in his name cheer us, He is the faithful "Amen."

198

Psalm C. L. M. *Tune "Old Hundred."*

All people that on earth do dwell,
Sing to the Lord with cheerful voice
Him serve with mirth, his praise forth tell,
Come ye before him and rejoice.

2 Know that the Lord is God indeed;
Without our aid he did us make:
We are his flock, he doth us feed,
And for his sheep he doth us take.

3 O enter then his gates with joy,
Within his courts his praise proclaim;
Let thankful songs your tongues employ,
O bless and magnify his name.

4 Because the Lord our God is good,
His mercy is forever sure;
His truth at all times firmly stood,
And shall from age to age endure.

199 Hear and Answer Prayer.

FANNY J. CROSBY. WM. J. KIRKPATRICK.

1. I am pray - ing, bless - ed Sav - iour, To be more and more like thee;
2. I am pray - ing, bless- ed Sav - iour, For a faith so clear and bright
3. I am pray - ing to be hum - bled By the power of grace di - vine,
4. I am pray - ing, bless- ed Sav - iour, And my constant prayer shall be
I am pray - ing that thy Spir - it Like a dove may rest on me.
That its eye will see thy glo - ry Thro' the deep - est, dark - est night.
To be clothed up - on with meekness, And to have no will but thine.
For a per - fect con - se - cra - tion, That shall make me more like thee.
CHORUS.
Thou who know-est all my weak-ness, Thou who knowest all my care,
While I plead each precious promise, Hear, oh, hear and answer prayer.

200

Psalm XCVI. C. M. *Tune "Azmon."*

O SING a new song to the Lord:
  Sing all the earth to God,
To God sing, bless his name, and show
  His saving health abroad.

2 Among the heathen nations all
  His glory do declare;
And unto all the people show
  His works that wondrous are.

3 The Lord is great, and greatly he
  Is to be magnified:
Yea, worthy to be feared is he
  Above all gods beside.

4 For all the gods are idols dumb,
  Which blinded nations fear;
But by Jehovah's mighty hand
  The heav'ns created were.

201 The Lord's Prayer.

Reverently.

A - men.

1. Our Father which art in heaven, hallowed | be thy | name, || Thy kingdom come, thy will be done in | earth, as-it | is in | heaven.

2. Give us this day our | daily | bread, || And forgive us our trespasses, as we forgive | them that | trespass a- | gainst us.

3. And lead us not into temptation, but deliver | us from | evil; || For thine is the kingdom, and the power and the | glory for- | ever and | ever. || A- | men.

202 Old Hundred. L. M.

DOXOLOGY. G. FRANC.

Praise God from whom all blessings flow; Praise him, all creatures here below;
Praise him a- bove, ye heav'nly host, Praise Father, Son and Ho- ly Ghost.

203 Gloria Patri.

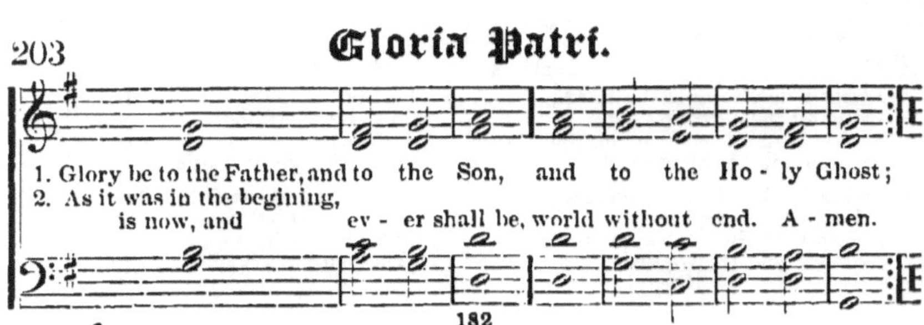
1. Glory be to the Father, and to the Son, and to the Ho - ly Ghost;
2. As it was in the begining, is now, and ev - er shall be, world without end. A - men.

SELECTIONS OF SCRIPTURE.

No 1. PSALM XXIII.

The Lord is my shepherd; I shall not want.

He maketh me to lie down in green pastures: he leadeth me beside the still waters.

He restoreth my soul: he leadeth me in the paths of righteousness for his name's sake.

Yea, though I walk through the valley of the shadow of death, I will fear no evil: for thou art with me; thy rod and thy staff they comfort me.

Thou preparest a table before me in the presence of mine enemies: thou anointest my head with oil; my cup runneth over.

Surely goodness and mercy shall follow me all the days of my life; and I will dwell in the house of the Lord for ever.

No 2. THE BEATITUDES.

Matt. v: 3-12.

Blessed are the poor in spirit:

For theirs is the kingdom of heaven.

Blessed are they that mourn:

For they shall be comforted.

Blessed are the meek:

For they shall inherit the earth.

Blessed are they which do hunger and thirst after righteousness:

For they shall be filled.

Blessed are the merciful:

For they shall obtain mercy.

Blessed are the pure in heart.

For they shall see God.

Blessed are the peacemakers:

For they shall be called the children of God.

Blessed are they which are persecuted for righteousness' sake:

For theirs is the kingdom of heaven.

Blessed are ye, when men shall revile you, and persecute you, and shall say all manner of evil against you falsely, for my sake.

Rejoice, and be exceeding glad: for great is your reward in heaven: for so persecuted they the prophets which were before you.

No 3. THE TEN COMMANDMENTS.

Exodus xx.

And God spake all these words, saying, I am the Lord thy God, which have brought thee out of the land of Egypt, out of the house of bondage.

FIRST.

Thou shalt have no other gods before me.

SECOND.

Thou shalt not make unto thee any graven image, or any likeness of any thing that is in heaven above, or that is in the earth beneath, or that is in the water under the earth: Thou shalt not bow down thyself to them, nor serve them: for I the Lord thy God am a jealous God, visiting the iniquity of the fathers upon the children unto the third and fourth generations of them that hate me; And shewing mercy unto thousands of them that love me, and keep my commandments.

THIRD.

Thou shalt not take the name of the Lord thy God in vain, for the Lord will not hold him guiltless that taketh his name in vain.

FOURTH.

Remember the sabbath-day, to keep it holy. Six days shalt thou labor, and do all thy work; But the seventh day is the sabbath of the Lord thy God: in it thou shalt not do any work, thou, nor thy son, nor thy daughter, thy man-servant, nor thy maid-servant, nor thy cattle, nor thy stranger that is within thy gates: For in six days the Lord made heaven and earth, the sea, and all that in them is, and rested the seventh day: wherefore the Lord blessed the sabbath-day, and hallowed it.

FIFTH.

Honor thy father and thy mother; that thy days may be long upon the land which the Lord thy God giveth thee.

SIXTH.

Thou shalt not kill.

SEVENTH.

Thou shalt not commit adultery.

EIGHTH.

Thou shalt not steal.

NINTH.

Thou shalt not bear false witness against thy neighbor.

TENTH.

Thou shalt not covet thy neighbor's house, thou shalt not covet thy neighbor's wife, nor his man-servant, nor his maid-servant, nor his ox, nor his ass, nor anything that is thy neighbor's.

No 4. PSALM I.

Blessed is the man that walketh not in the counsel of the ungodly, nor standeth in the way of sinners, nor sitteth in the seat of the scornful.

But his delight is in the law of the Lord; and in his law doth he meditate day and night.

And he shall be like a tree planted by the rivers of water, that bringeth forth his fruit in his season; his leaf also shall not wither; and whatsoever he doeth shall prosper.

The ungodly are not so: but are like the chaff which the wind driveth away.

Therefore the ungodly shall not stand in the judgment, nor sinners in the congregation of the righteous.

For the Lord knoweth the way of the righteous: but the way of the ungodly shall perish.

No 5. PSALM C.

Make a joyful noise unto the Lord, all ye lands.

Serve the Lord with gladness; come before his presence with singing.

Know ye that the Lord he is God: it is he that hath made us, and not we ourselves: we are his people, and the sheep of his pasture.

Enter into his gates with thanksgiving, and into his courts with praise: be thankful unto him, and bless his name.

For the Lord is good, his mercy is everlasting; and his truth endureth to all generations.

No 6. PRAISE.

Praise our God, all ye his servants, and ye that fear him, both small and great.

Both young men and maidens; old men and children:

Let them praise the name of the Lord: for his name alone is excellent; his glory is above the earth and heaven.

Let the people praise thee, O God; let all the people praise thee.

Let us come before his presence with thanksgiving, and make a joyful noise unto him with psalms.

I will bless the Lord at all times; his praise shall continually be in my mouth.

While I live will I praise the Lord:

I will sing praises unto my God while I have any being.

O come let us make a joyful noise unto the God of our salvation.

O Lord, open thou my lips; and my mouth shall show forth thy praise.

No 7. PRAYER.

The Lord is nigh unto all them that call upon him, to all that call upon him in truth.

Seek ye the Lord while he may be found, call ye upon him while he is near.

Then shall ye call upon me, and ye shall go and pray unto me, and I will hearken unto you.

Evening and morning and at noon will I pray.

Watch, and pray, that ye enter not into temptation.

Pray without ceasing. In everything give thanks.

Call upon me in the day of trouble: I will deliver thee.

Let us therefore come boldly unto the throne of grace, that we may obtain mercy, and find grace to help in time of need.

And whatsoever ye shall ask in my name, that will I do, that the Father may be glorified in the Son.

But thou, when thou prayest, enter into thy closet, and when thou hast shut thy door, pray to thy Father which is in secret; and thy Father which seeth in secret, shall reward thee openly.

After this manner therefore pray ye.

No 8. GOD'S WORD.

Thy word is a lamp unto my feet and a light unto my path.

And all thy children shall be taught of the Lord; and great shall be the peace of thy children.

The law of thy mouth is better unto me than thousands of gold and silver.

How sweet are thy words unto my taste! yea, sweeter than honey to my mouth!

Show me thy way, O Lord; teach me thy path.

The words that I speak unto you, they are spirit, and they are life.

Open thou mine eyes, that I may behold wondrous things out of thy law.

Thy word is very pure; therefore thy servant loveth it.

For the word of God is quick, and powerful, and sharper than any two-edged sword.

And take the helmet of salvation, and the sword of the Spirit, which is the word of God.

No 9. GIVING.

Freely ye have received, freely give.

For God loveth a cheerful giver.

Remember the words of the Lord Jesus, how he said, It is more blessed to give than to receive.

He that hath pity upon the poor lendeth to the Lord.

The liberal soul shall be made fat: and he that watereth shall be watered also himself.

If there be first a willing mind, it is accepted according to that a man hath, and not according to that he hath not.

Give, and it shall be given unto you; good measure, pressed down, and shaken together, and running over, shall men give into your bosom.

Of every man that giveth it willingly with his heart ye shall take my offering.

Honor the Lord with thy substance, and with the first fruits of all thine increase.

Blessed is he that considereth the poor: the Lord will deliver him in time of trouble.

No 10. SALVATION.

All have sinned, and come short of the glory of God:

The soul that sinneth, it shall die.

Believe on the Lord Jesus Christ, and thou shalt be saved.

Except ye be converted, and become as little children, ye shall not enter into the kingdom of heaven.

Behold the Lamb of God, which taketh away the sins of the world.

Come now, and let us reason together, saith the Lord: though your sins be as scarlet, they shall be as white as snow; though they be red like crimson, they shall be as wool.

And the blood of Jesus Christ his Son cleanseth from all sin.

For God so loved the world, that he gave his only begotten Son, that whosoever believeth in him should not perish, but have everlasting life.

Neither is there salvation in any other: for there is none other name under heaven given among men, whereby we must be saved.

Whosoever will, let him take of the water of life.

That whosoever shall call upon the name of the Lord, shall be saved.

No 11. PROMISES.

I love them that love me, and those that seek me early shall find me.

Come unto me, all ye that labor and are heavy-laden, and I will give you rest.

Honor thy father and thy mother; that thy days may be long upon the land which the Lord thy God giveth thee.

Lo, I am with you alway, even unto the end of the world.

In my Father's house are many mansions: if it were not so, I would have told you. I go to prepare a place for you. And if I go and prepare a place for you, I will come again, and receive you unto myself; that where I am, there ye may be also.

My sheep hear my voice, and I know them, and they follow me: And I give unto them eternal life; and they shall never perish, neither shall any man pluck them out of my hand.

To him that overcometh will I grant to sit with me in my throne, even as I also overcame, and am set down with my Father in his throne.

Ye shall seek me, and find me, when ye shall search for me with all your heart.

Even the youths shall faint and be weary, and the young men shall utterly fall; but they that wait upon the Lord shall renew their strength.

A new heart also will I give you, and a new spirit will I put within you; and I will take away the stony heart out of your flesh, and I will give you an heart of flesh.

No 12. MISSIONS.

And he said unto them, Go ye into all the world, and preach the gospel to every creature.

And how shall they believe in him of whom they have not heard? and how shall they hear without a preacher? and how shall they preach, except they be sent?

Ask of me, and I shall give thee the heathen for thine inheritance, and the uttermost parts of the earth for thy possession.

Teaching them to observe all things whatsoever I have commanded you: and, lo, I am with you alway, even unto the end of the world.

And this gospel of the kingdom shall be preached in all the world for a witness unto all nations: and then shall the end come.

Therefore said he unto them, The harvest truly is great, but the laborers are few.

The field is the world: the good seed are the children of the kingdom;

Pray ye therefore the Lord of the harvest that he will send forth laborers into his harvest.

He that goeth forth and weepeth, bearing precious seed, shall doubtless come again with rejoicing, bringing his sheaves with him.

And the Gentiles shall come to thy light, and kings to the brightness of thy rising.

No 13. TEMPTATION.

Your adversary the devil, as a roaring lion walketh about, seeking whom he may devour.

My son, if sinners entice thee, consent thou not.

Enter not into the path of the wicked, and go not in the way of evil men.

And lead us not into temptation, but deliver us from evil;

Watch and pray that ye enter not into temptation.

Resist the devil and he will flee from you.

The Lord knoweth how to deliver the godly out of temptations.

I pray not that thou shouldest take them out of the world, but that thou shouldest keep them from the evil.

God is faithful, who will not suffer you to be tempted above that ye are able; but will with the temptation also make a way to escape.

For in that he himself hath suffered being tempted, he is able to succor them that are tempted.

Blessed is the man that endureth temptation; for when he is tried, he shall receive the crown of life.

No 14. TEMPERANCE.

Wine is a mocker.
Strong drink is raging;
And whosoever is deceived thereby is not wise.
He that loveth pleasure shall be a poor man;
He that loveth wine and oil shall not be rich.
Be not among wine-bibbers;
Among riotous eaters of flesh.
For the drunkard and the glutton shall come to poverty;
Who hath woe?
Who hath sorrow?
Who hath contentions?
Who hath babblings?
Who hath wounds without cause?
Who hath redness of eyes?
They that tarry long at the wine;
They that go to seek mixed wine.

Look not thou upon the wine when it is red, when it giveth his color in the cup, when it moveth itself aright.

At the last it biteth like a serpent, and stingeth like an adder.

Touch not; taste not; handle not;

Now therefore beware, I pray thee, and drink not wine nor strong drink, and eat not any unclean thing.

But Daniel purposed in his heart that he would not defile himself with the portion of the king's meat, nor with the wine which he drank.

No. 15. THE DOOR OF MY LIPS.

RECITE. —Let the words of my mouth, and the meditation of my heart, be acceptable in thy sight, O Lord, my strength, and my Redeemer. Ps. xix: 14. For there is not a word in my tongue, but, lo, O Lord, thou knowest it altogether. Ps. cxxxix: 4.

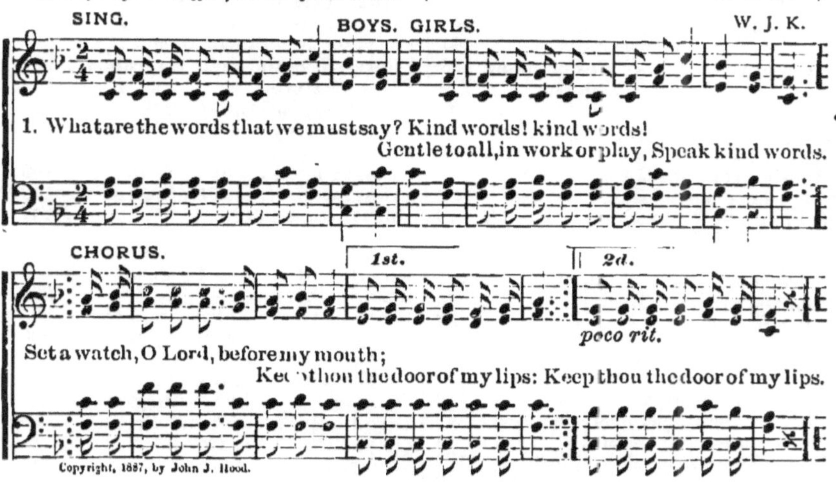

SING.
BOYS. GIRLS.
W. J. K.
1. What are the words that we must say? Kind words! kind words!
Gentle to all, in work or play, Speak kind words.
CHORUS.
1st.
2d.
poco rit.
Set a watch, O Lord, before my mouth;
Keep thou the door of my lips: Keep thou the door of my lips.

RECITE.—A soft answer turneth away wrath, but grievous words stir up anger. Prov. xv: 1.

2 What are the words that we must say?
True words! true words!
God's own command we must obey,
Speak true words.

CHO.—Set a watch, O Lord, before my [mouth;
Keep thou the door of my lips.:‖

RECITE.—The ninth commandment is, "Thou shalt not bear false witness against thy neighbor." Ex. xx: 16. Lying lips are abomination to the Lord, but they that deal truly are his delight. Prov. xii: 22.

3 What are the words that we must say?
Pure words! pure words!
Pure as the shining light of day;
Speak pure words.

CHO.—Set a watch, O Lord, before my [mouth;
Keep thou the door of my lips.:‖

RECITE.—The third commandment is, "Thou shalt not take the name of the Lord thy God in vain: for the Lord will not hold him guiltless that taketh his name in vain." Ex. xx: 7 Let no corrupt communication proceed out of your mouth. Eph. iv: 29.

4 What are the words that we must say?
Bright words! bright words!
Happy of heart as birds in May;
Speak bright words.

CHO.—Set a watch, O Lord, before my [mouth;
Keep thou the door of my lips.:‖

RECITE.—Pleasant words are as a honeycomb, sweet to the soul. Prov. xvi: 24. A word spoken in due season, how good is it. Prov. xv: 23.

5 What are the words that we must say?
Good words! good words!
Loving the Lord, we'll sing and pray;
Speak good words.

CHO.—Set a watch, O Lord, before my [mouth;
Keep thou the door of my lips.:‖

RECITE.—It is a good thing to give thanks unto the Lord, and to sing praise unto thy name, O most high. Ps. xcii: 1 Continue in prayer. Col. iv: 2. And whatsoever ye do, in word or deed, do all in the name of the Lord Jesus. Col. iii: 17.

CHO.—Set a watch, O Lord, defore my [mouth;
Keep thou the door of my lips.:‖

—E. E. Hewitt.

INDEX.

Titles in CAPITALS; First lines in Roman.

SELECTIONS OF SCRIPTURE.

www.ingramcontent.com/pod-product-compliance
Lightning Source LLC
Chambersburg PA
CBHW020244170426
43202CB00008B/214
9783337089795